Christmas Past &
Christmas Presents

Catherine Austin

A Sterling/Chapelle Book
® Sterling Publishing Co., Inc. New York

The photographs for this book were taken at
Anita Louise's Bear Lace Cottage, Park City, Utah;
Mary Gaskill's Trends & Traditions, Ogden, Utah;
The Beehive House, Salt Lake City, Utah;
and at the homes of
Penelope Hammons and Jo Packham.
Their cooperation and trust
are greatly appreciated.

10 9 8 7 6 5 4 3 2 1

A Sterling/Chapelle Book

First paperback edition published in 1994 by
Sterling Publishing Company, Inc.
387 Park Avenue South, New York, N.Y. 10016
© 1993 by Chapelle Ltd.
Distributed in Canada by Sterling Publishing
℅ Canadian Manda Group, P.O. Box 920, Station U
Toronto, Ontario, Canada M8Z 5P9
Distributed in Australia by Capricorn Link (Australia) Pty Ltd.
P.O. Box 704 , Windsor, NSW 2756, Australia
Printed and bound in China
All rights reserved

Sterling ISBN 1-4027-0097-0

Owners
Terrece Beesley
Jo Packham

Staff
Trice Boerens
Tina Annette Brady
Sheri Lynn Castle
Holly Fuller
Kristi Glissmeyer
Cherie Hanson
Susan Jorgensen
Margaret Shields Marti
Jackie McCowen
Barbara Milburn
Kathleen R. Montoya
Pamela Randall
Jennifer Roberts
Florence Stacey
Lew Stoddard
Nancy Whitley
Gloria Zirkel

Designers
Terrece Beesley
Trice Boerens
Holly Fuller
Ann Marie Groben
Mary Jo Hiney
Marlene Lund
Margaret Shields Marti
Jo Packham
Jennifer Roberts
Florence Stacey
Susan Whitelock
Mario Salas
of La Bouquetiere,
San Francisco

Photographer
Ryne Hazen

I'm giving you this
special gift and know
you'll understand why I'd
rather give you something
that I made myself
by hand.

From
a loving friend

CONTENTS

FOR THE ART CONNOISSEUR

FOR THE WRITER
Stenciled Throw — 10
Decorated Journal — 11
FOR THE PAINTER
Apron, Caddy & Paintbrushes — 15
FOR THE POET
Quilted Chair — 17
FOR THE MUSICIAN
Trinket Box — 21
FOR THE VICTORIAN LADY
Antique Oval Fan — 23
Beautiful Lady Fan — 26
Purple Button Fan — 28

FOR THE OUTDOORS ENTHUSIAST

FOR THE FISHERMAN
Supply Box — 32
Pinecone Firestarters — 34
FOR THE HUNTER
Cross-stitch Afghan — 35
FOR THE GARDEN PARTY LOVER
Bottle Labels — 41
Picnic Basket — 41
FOR THE GARDENER
Watering Cans — 47

FOR THE LEARNED

FOR THE TEACHER
Ribbon Apple — 50
FOR THE COLLECTOR
Santa Stocking — 51
FOR THE LAWYER
Desk Set — 59
FOR THE GOURMET COOK
Cooking Basket — 61
Wax Seals — 62
FOR THE LOVER OF NEEDLEWORK
Sewing Box — 64

FOR OUR FAMILY AND FRIENDS

FOR OUR DEAR FRIEND
Photo Frame — 70
FOR OUR DAUGHTER
Porcelain Doll — 73

FOR OUR SON
Quilted Stockings — 77
FOR OUR FATHER
Painted Goblets — 79
Needlepoint Coasters — 81
FOR OUR MOTHER
Hat Box & Mirror — 85
FOR OUR EGG-CENTRIC AUNT
Ribbon Egg — 89
FOR OUR GRANDDAUGHTER
Handkerchief Doll — 91
Ribbon Stocking — 95

FOR THE ROMANTIC

FOR THE PASTRY PUNDIT
Rose Cookies — 98
FOR THE ADVENTURER
Compass Box — 101
FOR THE COUTURIERE
Fruit Pincushions — 103
FOR THE LOVER OF BOOKS
Victorian Bookends — 109
FOR THE DESSERT LOVER
Dessert Cover — 111
FOR THE TEA PARTY LOVER
Fantasy Tea Set — 113

FOR THE GIFT-GIVER

GIFT TAGS FOR WRAPPING
Wrapped Present — 116
Fabric Envelope — 119
Velvet Hearts — 121
Clay Heart — 123
Tree Star — 125
HANDMADE CARDS FOR SENDING
Abacus Tree — 127
Lacy Basket — 129
Brass Stars — 131
FANCY BOXES FOR GIVING
Taffeta Boxes — 133
Pansy Box — 135
Velvet Bags — 137

GENERAL INSTRUCTIONS — 138

METRIC CHART — 143

INDEX — 144

Artists define the world with words, color and music. Offer a gift that reflects their unique insight. For the writer, give a velvet throw to keep warm while journal writing. For the painter, make a stenciled smock, paint caddy and colorful brushes. And for the poet, upholster a comfortable quilted chair. For the musician, decorate a small box with old sheet music. For the Victorian Lady, create dainty fans.

For The Art Connoisseur

CHAPTER

1

STENCILED THROW

MATERIALS

Photograph on page 8.

1¾ yards of floral print fabric
1¾ yards of purple velvet;
    matching thread
Acrylic paints: red, green,
    aqua, purple, brown
Manila folder
Sponge brushes

DIRECTIONS

1. Cut both floral print fabric and purple velvet 61" x 43". To make original stenciled pattern, trace floral print pattern from fabric and enlarge on copy machine. Make stencils from copy. Choose colors as desired.

2. To make stencils for throw pictured, make and transfer berry, flower and leaf patterns onto manila folder. Cut, using craft knife. Find patterns on pages 12 and 13.

3. Using sponge brush and working on large table, stencil patterns in colors desired. Position stencils as desired across fabric. Let paint dry.

4. With right sides facing, machine stitch floral print piece to stenciled purple velvet, leaving an opening to turn. Clip corners and turn. Slipstitch opening closed. Press from floral print side.

DECORATED JOURNAL

MATERIALS

Photograph on page 8.

10" x 3" strip of purple velvet
Acrylic paints: red, green,
    brown
Manila folder
Sponge brushes
½ yard of ¾" green
    plaid ribbon
½ yard of 1½" antique gold
    metallic ribbon
Six small gold medals or pins
½ yard of ½" red ribbon
½ yard of ¼" mauve beaded
    ribbon
Tacky glue

DIRECTIONS

1. To make stencil, make and transfer flower, leaf and berry patterns onto manila folder. Cut, using craft knife. Stencil red flower, green leaf and brown berries onto purple velvet strip as desired. Let paint dry.

2. Cut purple velvet strip at 45-degree angle on ends. Glue at diagonal to top of journal; see photograph. Glue one end inside front cover of journal and other end to back.

3. Glue green plaid ribbon horizontally across bottom of journal, securing ends inside.

4. Pin or glue medals to antique gold metallic ribbon. Glue ribbon length vertically to front of journal, securing ends inside cover; see photograph.

5. Glue red ribbon and mauve beaded ribbon at diagonal below and parallel to purple velvet strip.

'Tis a very old wish I've written before but my "Merry Christmas" never meant more

BERRY STENCIL

FLOWER STENCILS

12

LEAF STENCILS

13

FOR THE PAINTER

APRON, CADDY & PAINTBRUSHES

MATERIALS

Acrylic paints: green, purple,
    blue, lavender, yellow,
    forest green
Large sheet of plastic for
    stencils
Craft knife
Scrap of map board
Soft lead pencil
Paintbrushes
Dark green butcher apron
Wood craft caddy

DIRECTIONS

1. Cut three 6" x 9" sheets of plastic for stencils. To make stencils, place first plastic sheet over floral pattern on page 16. Cut all sections of Template 1. Repeat with second sheet and Template 2 patterns, and third sheet and Template 3 patterns.

2. Before painting apron, practice painting pansies on scratch paper. Paint apron by centering first stencil on pocket. Paint according to pattern, using purple, blue and lavender for petals. Use green for leaves. Center second stencil on pocket and paint. Center third stencil on pocket and paint.

3. Paint apron front; see photograph for placement. Paint petals using first stencil. Overlay with second stencil and paint, then overlay with third stencil and paint. Arrange pansies as desired, varying colors. Add leaves to fill in design.

4. Paint caddy forest green. Let paint dry. To complete caddy, use first pansy stencil and paint as desired. Overlay second stencil and paint petals, then overlay third stencil and paint petals. Arrange flowers as desired, varying colors. Add leaves to fill in design.

5. To color paintbrush handles, choose paints, then hold brush by bristles and dip brush handle into paint container. Repeat with remaining brushes and colors. If paint container is not deep enough, simply paint brush handles, using another paintbrush. Let paint dry.

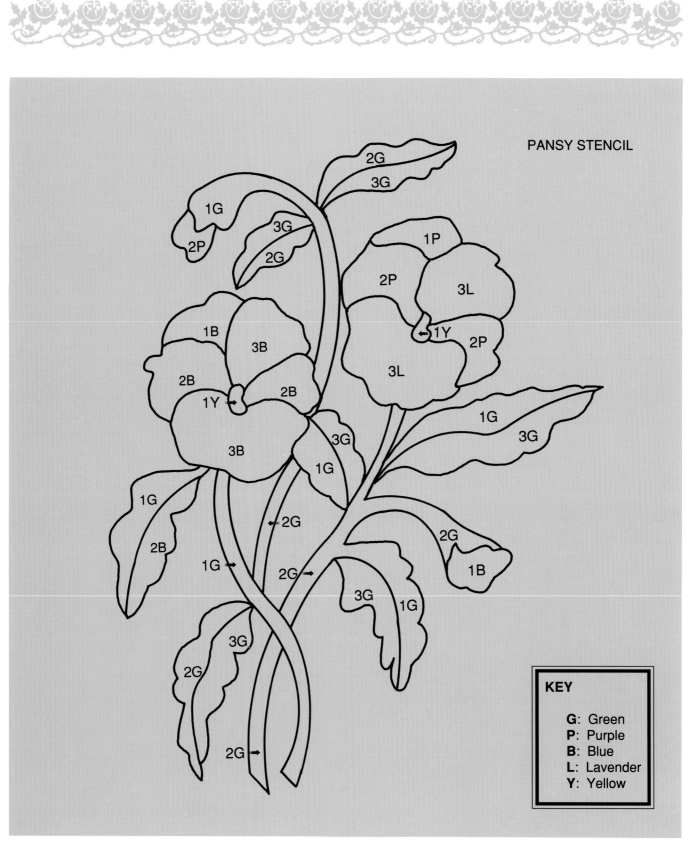

PANSY STENCIL

KEY

G: Green
P: Purple
B: Blue
L: Lavender
Y: Yellow

FOR THE POET

QUILTED CHAIR

MATERIALS

2 yards of rose fabric; matching thread
2 yards of floral print fabric
Green embroidery floss
Brass upholstery tacks
Green upholstery braid
General upholstery supplies

Pieced fabric in these directions will cover an 18" x 18" seat cushion and 12" x 12" chair back. All materials will need to be planned with consideration to your chair.

DIRECTIONS

1. Make Template A and Template B on page 19. From rose fabric, cut twenty-six Template As and forty Template Bs. From floral print fabric, cut forty Template As and twenty-six Template Bs.

2. Appliqué floral Template Bs to one corner of rose Template As, matching edges. Appliqué rose Template Bs to one corner of floral Template As.

3. To piece one section of seat cushion, join five appliquéd floral Template As and four appliquéd rose Template As, working in three rows of three; see Diagram A. Repeat to make four seat cushion sections alike. Join four sections with four floral Template Bs meeting to form circle in seat cushion center: see photograph.

Diagram A

17

4. To piece one section of chair back, join three appliquéd floral Template As and one appliquéd rose Template A, working in two rows of two; see Diagram B. Repeat to make four chair back sections alike. Join four sections with four appliquéd rose Template As meeting to form a circle in chair back center; see photograph. (Model shown in photograph has had additional blocks placed on outside edges to accommodate shape of back opening.)

5. Buttonhole stitch edge of rose Template Bs using two strands of green embroidery floss.

6. Adapt as needed by repeating pattern to prepare pieced seat cushion and chair back for upholstery. Use green braid and brass tacks to finish.

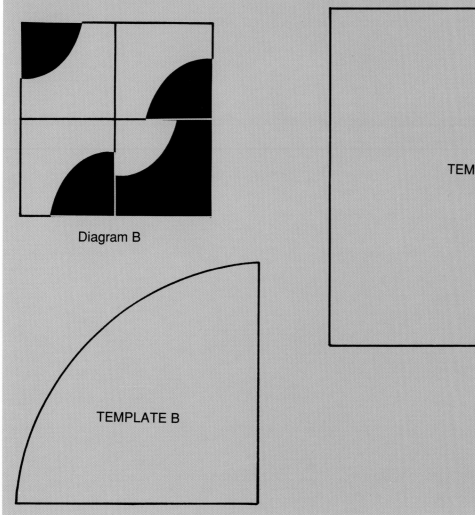

Diagram B

TEMPLATE A

TEMPLATE B

TRINKET BOX

MATERIALS

Rectangular wood box
   with lid
Old sheet music
Ivory acrylic paint
Paintbrush
Decoupage glue
Sheet of ivory paper
Black fine-point marker
Catalog and magazine cutouts
Brass musical note ornament
Black spray paint
Small white feather
2" black self-adhesive letters

DIRECTIONS

1. Paint box and lid ivory. Let paint dry.

2. Cut sheet music into pieces of varied sizes. Use decoupage glue to adhere sheet music pieces to painted box. Paint over box with decoupage glue. Let glue dry.

3. Make envelope pattern and transfer to ivory paper. Cut one. Fold and glue according to pattern. Also cut 2¾" x 3" piece from paper.

4. On 2¾" x 3" piece of paper and using black marker, write message "Sweetheart, if music be the food of Love, Play on!" Or write personal message.

5. From catalogs and magazines that carry music products, cut small album or cassette tape covers advertising favorite music.

6. On lid of box, glue ceramic musical note, envelope, message, feather and music cutouts as desired; see photograph.

7. Stick on black letters to spell "Jazz" or word of personal choice.

Sweetheart,
If music be
the food of Love,
Play on!

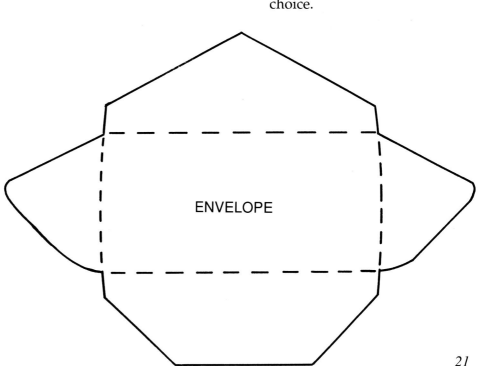

ENVELOPE

21

For The Victorian Lady

ANTIQUE OVAL FAN

MATERIALS

12" x 7" piece lightweight
   cardboard
7" square of peach fabric
   for front
7" square of light green
   fabric for back
4" square of textured pink
   fabric for oval
10" square of fleece
Two round toothpicks
   for handle
1 yard each of ⅛" pastel
   silk ribbon: peach, pink,
   green
2 yards of ⅛" ivory
   silk ribbon
¾ yard of ½" antique lace
6" length of ½" light green
   gathered satin ribbon
Seed beads: silver, peach,
   pink
Four small pearl beads
Silk embroidery thread: light
   green, pink, grey, mauve
Metallic gold embroidery
   thread
Two gold diamond-shaped
   filigree charms
Two gold swirl charms
9" length of ½" pink
   silk ribbon
6" length of ivory tatting
7" length of peach variegated
   wired ribbon for handle
Tacky glue

DIRECTIONS

See General Instructions to embroider bullion rosettes and make ribbon rosettes and leaves.

1. Make fan and oval patterns on page 25. Transfer patterns to lightweight cardboard. Using craft knife, cut two fans and one oval.

2. Make fan pattern again, adding ¼" seam allowance and omitting handle. Cut one from peach fabric and one from green fabric. Make oval pattern, adding ¼" seam allowance. From pink fabric, cut one.

3. Cut fleece to fit fan pattern and glue to one fan cardboard piece. Also, cut fleece to fit oval pattern and glue to cardboard oval.

4. Center fan cardboard piece, fleece side down, against wrong side of peach fabric. Wrap raw edges around cardboard. Glue fabric to cardboard back, clipping curves. Define scallops and curves of fan edge using fingernail, applying extra glue in those areas. Gently press with iron to smooth puckers.

5. Repeat Step 4, using oval cardboard piece and pink fabric. Repeat, using remaining fan cardboard piece and green fabric for back.

6. For ribbon hanger, measure 1" from top and from left side of fan back; mark. Measure 1" from top and from right side of fan back; mark. Puncture small hole at each mark. Cut ⅛" peach ribbon into 5" length, 13" length and 18" length. Insert 5" ribbon length through holes. Secure loose ends on wrong side of fan back with glue.

7. Glue toothpicks to handle of wrong side of fan back so that toothpick ends are even with bottom edge of handle. Set aside fan back .

8. Thread embroidery needle with 13" length of peach ribbon. Embroider four groups of three lazy daisy stitches to peach fan front. Sew pearl bead to each center. Sew silver seed bead to each petal end; see photograph.

9. Cut ivory ribbon into three 18" lengths. Using one length, outline fan front with loose, gathering stitch.

10. Sew gathering threads through antique lace. Gather to fit around fan. Glue seam allowance of lace along outer edge on wrong side of fan front. Cut green gathered ribbon into three equal lengths. Arch and glue seam allowance of each length at top and to wrong side of fan front; see photograph.

11. Make two rosettes using peach silk ribbon. Make four mauve rosette buds. Using pen, mark placement of rosettes; see photograph. Using pink, grey and green embroidery thread, stitch three bullion flowers with leaves in vertical line along right side of oval from bottom. Repeat on other side.

12. Using 18" length of ivory ribbon, stitch two fern fronds from bottom of oval; see photograph. Using mauve embroidery thread, stitch small rosebuds using lazy-daisy bullion stitch, placing them at random around oval.

13. Glue ribbon rosettes and buds in place. Cut green ribbon into two 18" lengths. Using one length, stitch ribbon leaves at base of rosettes, buds and bullion roses. Cascade metallic gold embroidery thread throughout roses around oval. Sew peach and pink seed beads at random around oval; see photograph.

14. Glue filigree fan to wrong side of oval along long edge. Repeat with remaining filigree fan and long edge. Glue gold swirl to wrong side of oval at top and another at bottom. Gather 9" length of ½" pink silk ribbon and glue seam allowance to wrong side of oval at top right. Glue tatting to wrong side around oval.

15. Glue fan front to back. Wrap handle with 7" length of peach variegated wired ribbon. Using remaining 18" lengths of pink, peach, green and ivory silk ribbons, tie them into bow. Tie knot in each ribbon tail. Glue bow to top of fan handle. Glue oval centered on fan front.

To make the second fan pictured in the photogragh on page 22 and the third fan pictured on page 29, purchase materials listed for Beautiful Lady Fan and Purple Button Fan. Use patterns on pages 27 and 28, and follow general directions given for Antique Oval Fan.

Use imagination and original embellishments to make each fan unique. Refer to General Instructions for ribbon rosettes, pencil violets, yo-yos, leaves, lazy-daisy stitch and bullion embroidery.

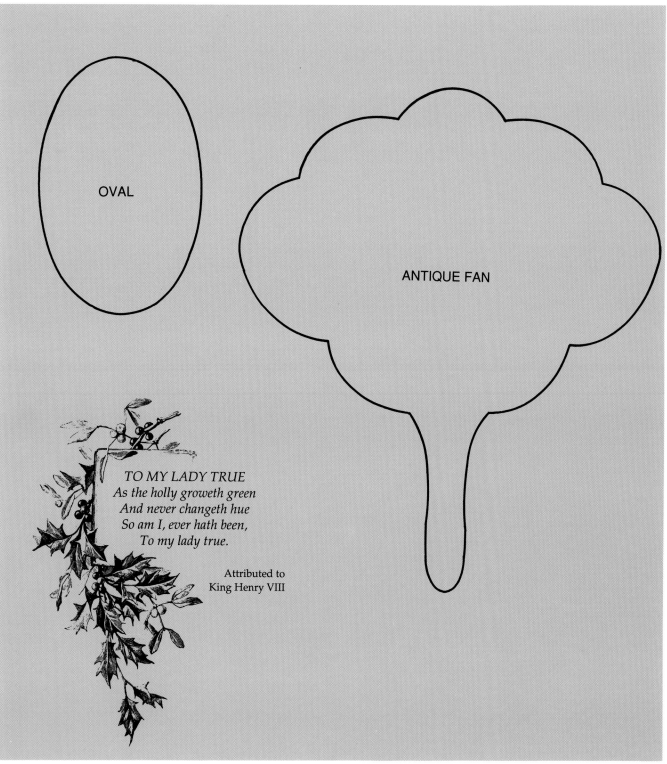

OVAL

ANTIQUE FAN

TO MY LADY TRUE
As the holly groweth green
And never changeth hue
So am I, ever hath been,
To my lady true.

Attributed to
King Henry VIII

BEAUTIFUL LADY FAN

MATERIALS

Photograph on page 22.

12" x 7" piece of lightweight
    cardboard
7" square of pink fabric for
    front
7" square of bridal lace for
    front
7" square of floral print fabric
    for back
7" square of fleece
Two round toothpicks for
    handle
4" length of ⅛" pink silk
    ribbon for hanger
12" x 1¼" strip of white
    chiffon

1 yard each of ¼" pastel silk
    ribbon: salmon, yellow for
    rosettes
15" lengths each of ¼" pastel
    silk ribbon: pink, blue for
    rosettes and pencil violets
¼ yard each of ⅛" silk ribbon:
    six pastel shades for
    small rosettes
Light green silk embroidery
    thread for bullion rosettes
1 yard of ⅛" light green silk
    ribbon for ferns
¼ yard each of ⅛" silk ribbon:
    dark salmon, aqua, light
    aqua for lazy daisy flowers
½ yard of ⅛" light blue silk
    ribbon to cascade

15" length of ¾" ivory tatting
    for trim
7" length of ½" green
    variegated wired ribbon
    for handle
7" length of 1" pink silk ribbon
    for large bow
Old greeting card cutout
Silver seed beads
Pearl sequins
Three small pearl beads for
    flower middles
Tacky glue

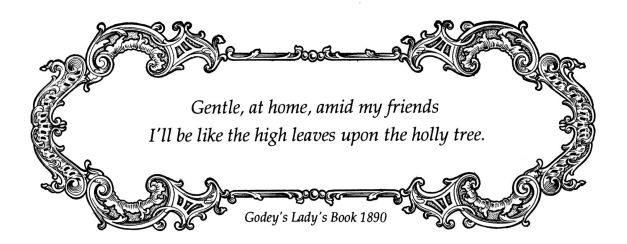

*Gentle, at home, amid my friends
I'll be like the high leaves upon the holly tree.*

Godey's Lady's Book 1890

LADY FAN

PURPLE BUTTON FAN

MATERIALS

12" x 7" piece of lightweight cardboard

7" square of purple fabric for front

7" square of floral print fabric for back

7" square of fleece

Two round toothpicks for handle

5" length of narrow ribbon for hanger

1" x 26" strip of fabric for ruffle

5" length of ½" lace

Fabric scraps in five colors cut into 2" circles for yo-yos

9" length of pink ¼" silk ribbon for rosette

Three different colors of ⅛" silk ribbon in 5" lengths each for small rosettes

4½" length of dark green ½" wired ribbon for leaf

Scrap of green fabric cut in 2" circle for leaf

½ yard of green ⅛" silk ribbon to cascade

12½" length of ½" ivory trim

7" length of ½" purple wired ribbon for handle

1½" x 6" piece of pink satin fabric for bow

1" x 10" strip of purple chiffon for fabric rose

½ yard each in four colors of ⅛" silk ribbon for bows

Small beads to decorate tails of bows

Assorted small antique buttons

Gold hand charm

Tacky glue

PURPLE FAN

Not much short of these gifts can tempt a nature worshiper to come in from the great outdoors. The angler can warm up indoors with pinecone firestarters and stash favorite fishing flies in a homemade box. When the hunter wants a rest, cover him in a cross-stitched elk afghan. The woman who adores garden parties will cherish a vintage picnic basket complete with personalized wine bottles. And the gardener's watering pitchers look as lively as the flower patch.

For The Outdoor Enthusiast

CHAPTER

2

FOR THE FISHERMAN

SUPPLY BOX

MATERIALS

Photographs on pages 30 and 33.

Wood box with lid
Masking tape
Acrylic paints: tan, brown
Paintbrushes
Paint sponge
Black fine-tip permanent
    marker
Spray adhesive
Fishing fly
Tacky glue

DIRECTIONS

1. Using tan paint, paint ¾" border along lid and vertically on corners of box. Paint edges of lid. Do not paint border on rear top of lid. To get straight edge, place masking tape ¾" from edge of lid and box. Paint area below straight tape edge. Let paint dry.

2. With black marker, write "fish" at 1" intervals across tan border.

3. Find line drawings in book of clip art or use fish patterns provided. Make as many copies of fish as desired to cover box and lid. Using spray adhesive, attach fish at random to lid and side of box. Glue largest fish inside center of lid.

4. Dilute small amount of brown paint with water. Using sponge, wash inside and outside of box with diluted paint, covering fish. Wipe excess paint with clean cloth. Let paint dry.

5. Using tacky glue, attach fishing fly near mouth of fish on inside lid of box.

PINECONE FIRESTARTERS

MATERIALS

Photograph on page 30.

Newspaper
Four boxes of paraffin
Double boiler or electric
    fry pan
Wax coloring chips or wax
    crayons
Scented oil for candles
24 medium-sized pinecones
Muffin tin
Vegetable oil
24 candle wicks, each 6" long
Basket

DIRECTIONS

1. Cover work area with newspaper. Melt paraffin in double boiler over hot water or in can placed in an electric fry pan filled with water. Add coloring chips and scented oil drops as desired.

2. Holding pinecones with tongs, dip cones into paraffin. Set cones upright on newspaper, allowing paraffin to harden. For thicker wax coating, make pinecones in cool place such as garage or outdoors in cool weather.

3. Lightly oil muffin cups with vegetable oil. Fill each cup half full with paraffin. While paraffin is still liquid, place one end of wick in each cup, leaving other end free. Place pinecone upright in each cup; allow paraffin to harden. Place muffin tin in freezer for a few minutes. Then, remove firestarters from cups. Arrange them in basket.

FOR THE HUNTER

CROSS-STITCH AFGHAN

MATERIALS

Photograph on page 36.

Completed cross-stitch on
   Vanessa-Ann Afghan
   Weave Fabric, 18 count
Yarn description: Worsted
   weight nubby yarn
   (50 gr. ball): 7 balls
   brown/grey/blue blend
Cotton crochet thread #5
   (5 gr., 25m. skein): 3 skeins
   light beige.
DMC Pearl Cotton #5 (5 gr.,
   25m. skein): 3 skeins #841
Size G crochet hook
Size 7 steel crochet hook
Size 18 tapestry needle

GAUGE
Approximately 8 sc and
   3 rows dec = 2"

DIRECTIONS

1. Fabric preparation: Trim sides so designs match (8 full patterns plus part of 2 patterns x 7 full patterns plus part of 2 patterns). The finished fabric size will be approximately 48" x 55" before crocheted edge. Crocheted edge will be approximately 4½" wide.

2. Machine zigzag stitch around entire outside edge of fabric. Turn ¼" under for hem and work over this hem. With crochet thread and size 7 hook, begin in any corner with 5 sc, (sk 3 threads of fabric, sc bet threads) around entire afghan, having 5 sc in ea corner, end with sl st in beg sc. Fasten off.

3. Edging: With G hook and yarn * ch 217, place a safety pin in last ch made for corner marker, ch 193, place a safety pin in last ch made for corner, rep from * once, join with sl st to beg ch, take care not to twist chain.

4. Note: Move marker pins up in corner sp at completion of ea corner.

Rnd 1: Ch 1, * sc in ea st to marked st, (sc, ch 1, sc) in marked st for corner, rep from * around, end with sl st in beg ch.

Rnd 2: Sl st backward into corner ch-1 sp, ch 4 for beg dc and ch 1, 2 dc in same sp, * dc in ea st to corner ch-1 sp, ch 4 for beg dc and ch 1, 2 dc in same sp, * dc in ea st to corner ch-1 sp, (2 dc, ch 1, 2 dc) in corner sp, rep from * around, end with dc in beg corner sp, sl st in 3rd ch of beg ch-4.

Rnd 3: Sl st into corner ch-1 sp, ch 4 for beg dc and ch 1, 2 dc in same sp, * (ch 2, sk next 2 sts, dc in ea of next 2 sts) across to corner sp, ch 2, (2 dc, ch 1, 2 dc) in corner ch-1 sp, rep from * around, end with dc in beg corner sp, sl st in 3rd ch of beg ch-4.

Rnd 4: Sl st into corner ch-1 sp, ch 4 for beg dc and ch 1, 2 dc in same sp, * (ch 2, 2 dc in next ch-2 sp) across to corner sp, ch 2 (2 dc, ch 1, 2 dc) in corner ch-1 sp, rep from * around, end with dc in beg corner sp, sl st in 3rd ch of beg ch-4.

Rnd 5: Sl st into corner ch-1 sp, ch 4 for beg dc and ch 1, 2 dc in same sp, * (dc in ea of next 2 dc, * * 2 dc in next ch-2 sp) across to corner ch-1 sp, end at * * (2 dc, ch 1, 2 dc) in corner sp, rep from * around, end with dc in beg corner ch-1 sp, sl st in 3rd ch of beg ch-4.

Rnd 6: Sl st into corner ch-1 sp, ch 7, sl st in 3rd ch from hook for picot, ch 1, 2 dc in same sp, [ch 3, sk next 3 sts, sc bet 3rd and 4th sts, * ch 3, sk next 4 sts, (2 dc, ch 3, sl st in top of last dc worked for picot, 2 dc) = picot shell, bet 4th and 5th sts, ch 3, sk next 4 sts, sc bet 4th and 5th sts from last picot shell, rep from * to corner, ch 3, * * (2 dc, ch 4 picot, ch 1, 2 dc) in corner ch-1 sp] rep bet [ ] around, end last rep at * *, dc in beg corner ch-1 sp, sl st in 3rd ch of beg ch 7. Fasten off.

5. Assembly: Pin corners and half-way points of edging to fabric, easing in fullness where necessary. With double strand of crochet thread, whip-stitch edging to fabric.

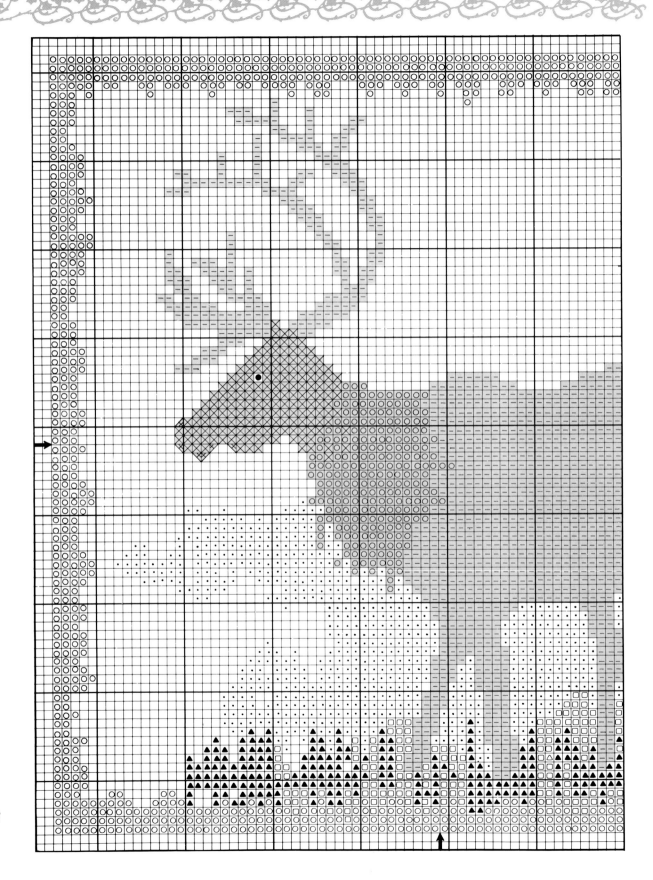

MODEL

Photograph on page 36.

Stitched on Vanessa-Ann Afghan Weave 18 over 1 thread, the finished design size is 4⅞" x 4⅞". The fabric was cut 49" x 58". Stitch design in every other square, alternating with each row; see photograph.

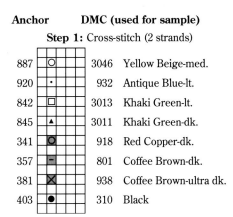

Anchor		DMC	(used for sample)
	Step 1: Cross-stitch (2 strands)		
887	○	3046	Yellow Beige-med.
920	·	932	Antique Blue-lt.
842	□	3013	Khaki Green-lt.
845	▲	3011	Khaki Green-dk.
341	◉	918	Red Copper-dk.
357	▦	801	Coffee Brown-dk.
381	✕	938	Coffee Brown-ultra dk.
403	●	310	Black

STITCH COUNT 88 X 88

FOR THE GARDEN PARTY LOVER

BOTTLE LABELS

MATERIALS

Photograph on page 43.

Three fancy beverage bottles
Two sheets heavy linen paper
Colored pencils
Spray adhesive

DIRECTIONS

To make waxed label pictured on page 40, see Wax Seals (Option 2) on page 63.

1. Using copy machine, copy bottle label patterns on pages 44 and 45 onto heavy linen paper. Color with pencils as desired. Cut labels. Attach to bottles with spray adhesive.

PICNIC BASKET

MATERIALS

Medium-sized picnic basket with lid
5' x 4' piece of matboard
2 yards rose velveteen
Polyester batting
Hot glue gun and glue sticks
2 yards of 1½" ivory lace
3 yards of 1" grey ribbon
¾ yard of green satin
2 yards of 1" rose ribbon
2" x 50" strip of ivory crochet
Large rectangular doily
Four small crochet doilies
Satin scraps: rose, peach, beige
String of faux pearls
White silk rosebud
Tablecloth with stitched floral design
2 yards of ¼" black satin ribbon
3½ yards of 1" peach/ivory crochet trim
1 yard of ¾" rose satin ribbon
1½ yards of 1" dark rose velveteen ribbon
1½ yards of 1" lace
Large crochet tablerunner
1½ yards of ⅜" ivory satin ribbon
Linen envelope

DIRECTIONS

See General Directions to make fabric rosettes and rosebuds.

1. Measure inside basket bottom and cut one piece of matboard to fit. Trim edges so matboard fits easily inside basket. Measure basket lid and cut one matboard piece to fit. Then, subtract 1" from all edges of basket lid measurement and cut one matboard piece to go inside lid.

2. Cut piece of velveteen to fit bottom matboard, adding 2" to all edges. Cut four pieces of batting, using matboard piece as pattern. Glue batting to matboard. Center matboard, batting side down, on wrong side of velveteen. Wrap fabric around to back and glue. Set aside.

3. Cut rectangle from velveteen to line inside of basket, measuring horizontally from left side, down across basket bottom, and up right side for rectangle's width. Measure vertically from back, down across basket bottom and up front for rectangle's width. Cut one rectangle.

4. Glue long raw edge of velveteen to top inside edge of basket back. Smooth velveteen along long sides of inner basket, gathering excess at corners. Glue remaining raw edges to top inside edge of basket front.

5. Glue velveteen-covered matboard to inside bottom of basket with raw edges down.

6. Measure around top edge of basket. Cut 1½" lace to fit. Glue lace along top edge of basket and lining, covering raw edges of velveteen.

7. Measure around inside basket lid and cut grey ribbon to measurements. Glue ribbon around inside edge of basket lid.

8. Cut piece of green satin to fit remaining lid matboard, adding 2" to all edges. Cut four pieces of batting, using matboard piece as pattern. Glue batting to matboard. Center matboard, batting side down, on wrong side of satin. Wrap fabric around to back and glue.

9. Cut four 6" squares of rose velveteen. Fold each square in half diagonally to make four triangles. Fit one triangle to each corner of satin-covered matboard. Cut two 3" lengths

of 1" rose ribbon. Fold each into V-shape. Glue raw ends of each V-shape under velveteen corners; see photograph.

10. Center satin-covered matboard on inside basket lid and glue.

11. Measure around lid matboard. Cut length of 1" rose ribbon to fit around matboard. Glue. Cut strip of ivory crochet trim to fit over rose ribbon. Apply liquid ravel preventer to edges. Glue in

place. Cut center from large rectangular doily, leaving about 1" border. Glue inside ivory crochet trim; see photograph.

12. Layer piece of rose velveteen and three doilies. Glue to center of inside lid.

13. Make two 2" green satin rosettes, one 2" rose satin rosette, one 2" peach satin rosette, one 1" beige satin rosette and three green satin rosebuds.

14. Set one 2" green rosette aside. Gather all other satin flowers, scraps of lace, faux pearls and white silk rosebud. Arrange in bouquet; see photograph. Add bow made from ¾" rose satin ribbon. Glue to center of inside lid.

15. From stitched floral tablecloth, cut piece to fit remaining matboard, adding 2" to all edges and centering design. Cut four pieces of batting, using matboard as pattern. Glue batting to matboard. Center matboard, batting side down, on wrong side of floral tablecloth. Wrap fabric around; glue. Set aside.

16. Glue covered matboard to basket lid top. Frame stitched floral design with ¼" black satin ribbon as desired.

17. Cut peach/ivory crochet border to fit edge of basket top lid, bottom edge of basket and outer edge of handles; see photograph. Glue.

18. Cut two lengths of 1" lace ribbon to fit inside of basket handles. Glue.

19. From tablerunner, cut strip of crochet wide enough to fit around outside of basket, and 2" shorter than total height of basket. Glue in place, 2" from top edge of basket; see photograph.

20. Cut length of rose velveteen ribbon to fit around outside of basket. Glue in place, 2" from top edge of basket, overlapping crochet tablerunner; see photograph.

21. Cut 2" strip of ivory crochet to fit top outside edge of basket. Glue. Cut and glue crochet around handles as needed.

22. Cut two 24" lengths of ivory satin ribbon. Stitch end of each ribbon length to top corners of linen envelope. Sit envelope in

basket, front forward. Thread ribbons around hinges between basket and lid. Secure with bow.

23. Cut two 12" lengths of black satin ribbon. Stitch ends of ribbons to inside basket lid and inside basket top to make ribbon hinges. Remaining black ribbon can be used to embellish inside basket lid.

24. Glue remaining green satin rosette to front center of basket over 2" crochet strip.

BOTTLE LABEL

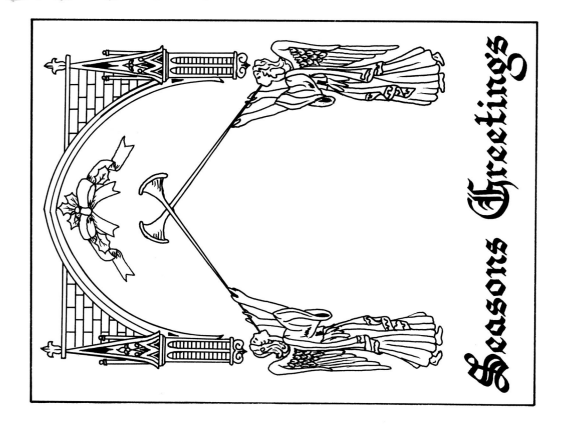

BOTTLE LABELS

FOR THE GARDENER

WATERING CANS

MATERIALS

12"-tall metal watering can
  with handle
9"-tall metal watering can
  with handle
Metal primer spray paint
Acrylic paints: white, dark
  green, light green, pink,
  yellow, red, purple
Flat spray glaze

DIRECTIONS

1. Spray watering cans with
metal primer. Let primer dry.

2. Paint cans and handles
white. Let paint dry.

3. Paint dark green vertical
stripes of varying lengths
from top of can all around; see
photograph. Let paint dry.

4. Paint light green squiggly
lines on top of green stripes.
Let paint dry.

5. Paint pink, yellow, red and
purple dots on top of light
green lines to look like
flowers; see photograph. Let
paint dry.

6. Spray cans with flat glaze.
Let glaze dry.

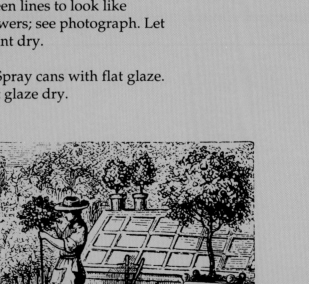

They study and share their knowledge with others. To let the learned know they are appreciated, start by giving a teacher a ribbon-adorned apple that won't spoil. The collector can display a porcelain St. Nick tucked into a velvet stocking. A handsome painted desk set should tidy any professional desk. The gourmet cook can fill an embroidered basket with fancy edibles and wax-sealed bottles. Those who can't get enough of needlework can store their tools in a multifaceted sewing box.

For The Learned

RIBBON APPLE

MATERIALS
Photograph on page 48.

3" plastic craft apple
9" x 5" piece of fleece
9" x 5" piece of burgundy
    satin; matching thread
⅛" silk ribbon: five pink
    shades, ⅝ yard each
⅛" silk ribbon: two green
    shades, ⅝ yard each
1 yard of ⅛" green silk ribbon
Silk embroidery thread: two
    green shades
Mauve metallic seed beads
6" length of gold cording
12" length of 1" ivory lace
12" length of 1" burgundy
    wired ribbon
15" length of 1" dark green
    wired ribbon

DIRECTIONS

*See General Instructions to
embroider lazy-daisy leaves and
to make ribbon rosettes and
leaves.*

1. Glue fleece to apple as
smoothly as possible. Trim
excess.

2. Fold satin in half, with right
sides facing and short ends
aligned, stitching ¼" seam.
Press seam open. Turn and
slip fabric tube over apple.
Fold top edge down ¼" and
sew gathering thread around
edge; see Diagram A. Pull
thread tightly to gather and
secure. Glue gathered satin to
apple and smooth. Repeat
with bottom edge.

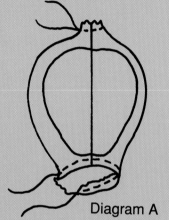
Diagram A

3. Cut ⅛" pink silk ribbon into
sixteen 5" lengths and make
sixteen rosettes. To place
rosettes, measure 1½" from top
of apple. Lightly mark eight
places an equal distance from
each other around apple.
Repeat, measuring 2½" from
top, marking between previous
marks; see Diagram B. Glue
rosettes on marks.

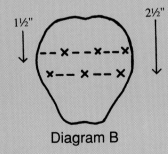
Diagram B

4. Alternating two green
shades of ⅛" silk ribbon, use
lazy-daisy stitch to embroider
leaves near rosettes. Also lazy-
daisy stitch small leaves with
silk embroidery thread. Place
leaves randomly around
rosettes, alternating with two
green shades of thread. Scatter
seed beads in same manner.
For hanger, loop gold cording,
knotting ends. Glue knot to
center of apple top.

5. To make lace and ribbon
ruffled circles, fold 12" length
of 1" lace in half. With right
sides facing and short edges
aligned, glue or stitch small
seam. Turn. Stitch gathering
thread around straight edge of
lace. Pull thread tightly to
gather, leaving small center
opening. Place lace circle on
top of apple, carefully
threading hanger through
center opening. Repeat, using
12" of burgundy wired ribbon,
gluing ribbon ruffled circle to
lace circle.

6. Cut three 5" lengths of dark
green wired ribbon and make
ribbon leaves. Glue two leaves
to right side of apple near
center, and one to left side of
apple.

SANTA STOCKING

MATERIALS
Photograph on page 52.

2"-tall porcelain Santa
   Claus head
¼ yard of red fabric; matching
   thread
¼ yard of black polished
   cotton
Polyester stuffing
Tacky glue
½ yard of taupe satin fabric;
   matching thread
3" length of ½" elastic
Small snap
Hook and eye set
1 yard of burgundy velvet;
   matching thread
1 yard of burgundy satin
1 yard of ¼" burgundy and
   gold trim
½ yard of ¾" burgundy and
   gold trim
2 yards of ¼" burgundy velvet
   ribbon
1½ yards of ¼" cording
Burgundy seed beads
Beading needle
20" length of burgundy satin
   ribbon
Small artificial tree

DIRECTIONS (for body)
All seams are ¼".

1. Make body pattern on page
54. From red fabric, cut two
body pieces. Also cut four
4¼" x 1¾" rectangles for arms.
From black fabric, cut four
2¼" x 1¾" rectangles for
mittens. Then, cut four mitten
shapes; see diagram.

1¾"

2¼"

Diagram

2. Stitch wrist of one mitten
piece to lower edge of each
arm piece. Match two arm/
mitten pieces with right sides
facing and stitch, leaving
small opening. Clip between
thumb and hand on mittens.
Turn. Stuff moderately.
Slipstitch opening closed.
Repeat for second arm. Set
aside.

3. With right sides facing,
stitch body, leaving opening at
top for neck. Turn. Stuff body
firmly. Fold raw edge of neck
under ¼" and stitch gathering
thread along edge. Insert
porcelain head. Pull threads
tightly around neck; secure
with glue. Stitch arms to body.

DIRECTIONS (for underdressing)

1. Make underdressing
patterns on page 55. From
taupe satin fabric, cut one
front and two backs. Cut 1¼"
x 8" strip for belt and 1" x 5"
bias strip for neck binding.

2. With right sides facing and
raw edges aligned, stitch back
pieces at center back, stopping
2" below neck; backstitch. Fold
raw edges of opening under.
With right sides of back and
front pieces facing, stitch
shoulders, sleeve and side
seams. Fold tucks on shoulder
seam to wrong side of
garment; stitch.

3. With right sides of bias strip
and undergarment facing,
stitch around neck. Double
fold strip to wrong side of
garment; slipstitch. Place
undergarment on Santa body.
Pull center back pieces tightly
around neck; stitch along bias
strip. Stitch ¼" hem in edge of
wrists and bottom of
undergarment.

4. Fold belt piece with right
sides facing to measure ⅝".
Stitch long edge and one short
edge. Turn. Slipstitch opening
closed. Fit belt snugly around
waist. Mark placement on belt
for hook and eye; attach.

DIRECTIONS (for robe)

1. Make robe patterns on page 56. From velvet, cut one back and two fronts. Make lining patterns on page 56. From satin, cut one lining back piece on fold. Also, cut one right front piece, then flip and cut one left front piece.

2. With right sides of robe front and back facing, stitch shoulders, sleeves and side seams. Fold tucks on shoulder seam to wrong side of robe; see pattern. Stitch to secure at seam allowance. Repeat for robe lining.

3. With right sides of robe and lining facing, stitch along front, around neck and along bottom, leaving small opening at bottom. Clip seam allowance at neck. Turn. Slipstitch opening closed. Fold raw edges under on sleeve of robe and lining; slipstitch. Repeat on other sleeve.

4. Place robe on Santa body. Fold lapels ¾" to front. Tie knots at ends of gold and burgundy trim. Wrap trim around waist and knot.

DIRECTIONS (for stocking)

1. Make stocking pattern on page 57. From burgundy velvet, cut two. Repeat, using burgundy satin for lining. Also from satin, cut 4½" x 25" piece for ruffle, 2" x 6" piece for hanger and 1½" bias strips, piecing as needed to equal 26". Make corded piping; set aside.

2. Stitch piping around sides and bottom of stocking front. With right sides facing, stitch stocking front to back on stitching line of piping, leaving top edge open. Clip curves. Turn.

3. With right sides facing, stitch ends of ruffle piece. Fold with wrong sides facing. Stitch gathering thread on long edge. Pull thread tightly to gather ruffle to fit top of stocking. Baste to stocking top. Fold hanger piece lengthwise with right sides facing. Stitch long edge. Turn. Fold piece in half, matching raw edges and leaving seam inside.

4. With right sides facing and edges aligned, stitch lining front and back leaving top edge and small seam above heal open. Slide lining over stocking, right sides facing and aligning seams at top edges. Stitch, catching hanger in seam. Turn through opening in lining. Slipstitch opening closed. Fold lining inside stocking.

5. Slipstitch gold trim to top edge of stocking along seamline. With velvet ribbon, make eight 2" loops, leaving long tails; secure. Tack loops at top of seam on toe side of stocking. Using 20" length of ribbon, make bow with long tails. Stitch to cover bottom loops. Twist and tack tails to stocking; see photograph.

6. String four 9" strands of beads. Stitch beads to ribbon and stocking; see photograph. Stuff stocking about half full. Place dressed Santa and small artificial tree inside stocking. With 20" length of satin ribbon, tie trim on Santa to stocking hanger. Tie ribbon into bow.

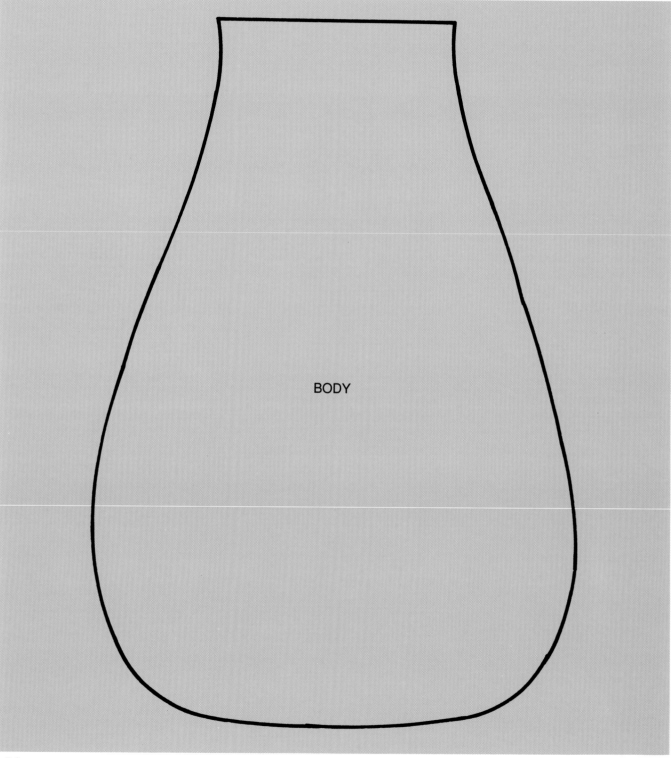

BODY

54

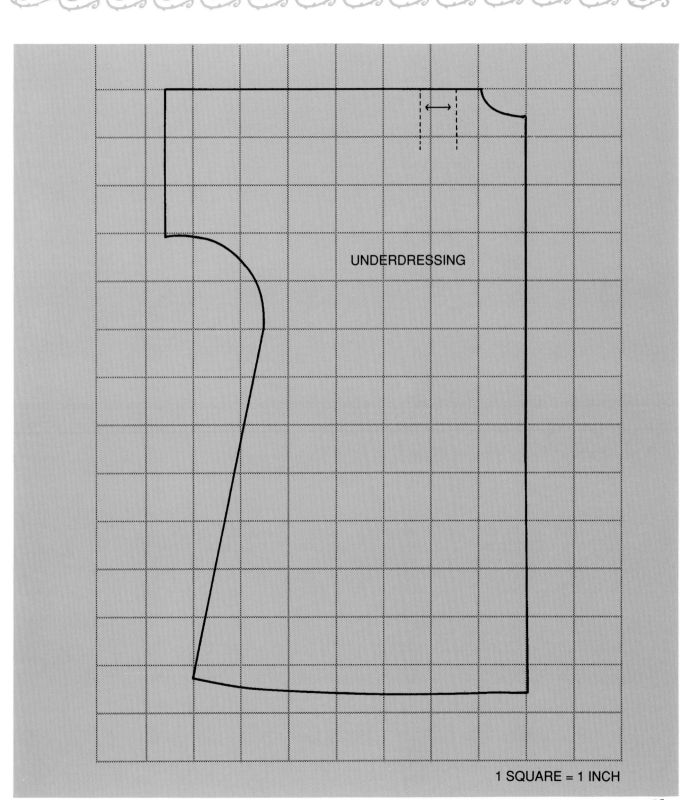

UNDERDRESSING

1 SQUARE = 1 INCH

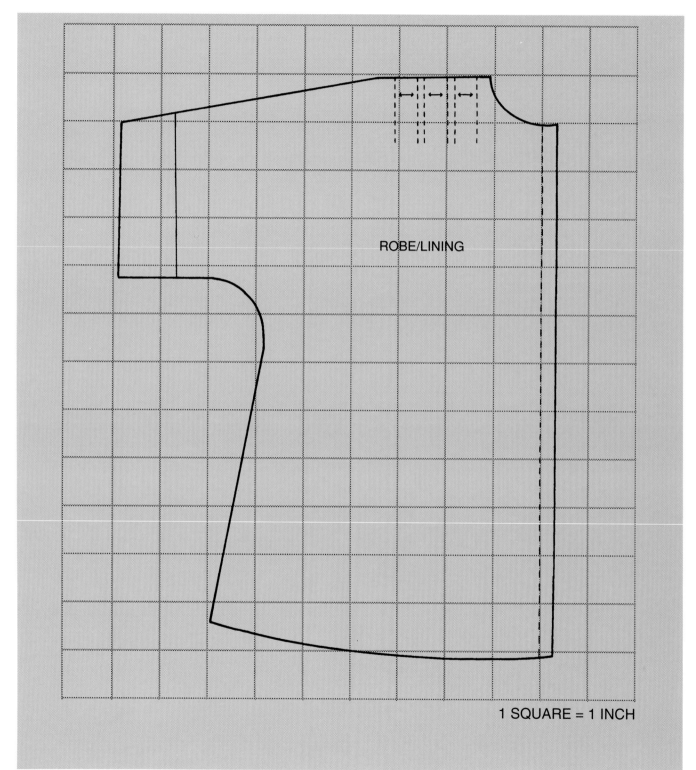

ROBE/LINING

1 SQUARE = 1 INCH

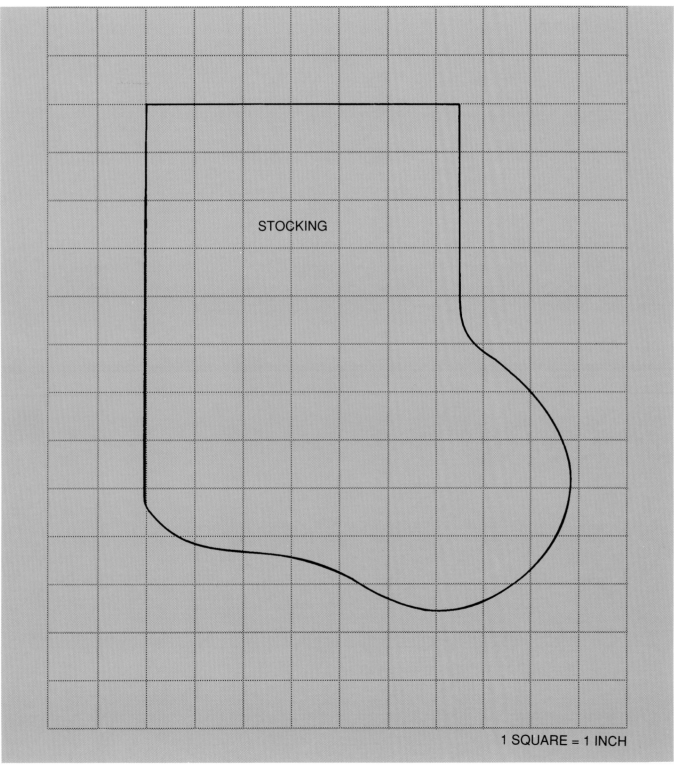

STOCKING

1 SQUARE = 1 INCH

FOR THE LAWYER

DESK SET

MATERIALS

Finished wood desk set
Acrylic paints: light green,
    lavender, brown, tan,
    peach, dark green,
    light brown
Paintbrushes

DIRECTIONS

1. Paint band of desk set
pieces light green. Let paint
dry. Measure ¾" from top of
light green block. Mark with
pencil. Draw line around desk
set piece, making ¾" border.
Paint this border lavender. Let
paint dry.

2. Trace acorn pattern. Using
scrap of carbon paper, transfer
the pattern to front of desk set
piece centered on light green
area. Paint acorns and leaves
as desired; see photograph.
Let paint dry.

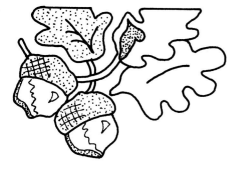

ACORNS

*May you know peace
at this Christmas time.*

For The Gourmet Cook

COOKING BASKET

MATERIALS

Medium-sized basket with
    handle
Purchased embroidered
    tablecloth; matching thread
Hot glue gun and glue sticks
2 yards of ½" white trim
6" x 4" oval cardboard cutout
Polyester batting
7½"-round lace doily
Liquid ravel preventer
Scraps of white crochet trim
2½ yards of 2" aqua ribbon
1 yard of 2" mauve ribbon

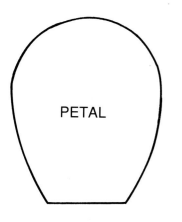

PETAL

DIRECTIONS

1. Measure length and width of basket. Consider design on tablecloth in planning how to cut two pieces for basket. Adding 1" to each measurement, cut piece from tablecloth to line basket. Then, cut 7" x 5" oval from remaining embroidered fabric.

2. Glue lining to top edge of basket. Trim excess fabric. Glue white trim along top edge of basket and lining, covering raw edges.

3. Cut four pieces of batting, using cardboard oval as pattern. Glue batting to cardboard.

4. Center cardboard oval, batting side down, on wrong side of fabric oval. Wrap fabric around to back and glue. Cut decorative center from lace doily. Glue remaining doily outline to back of oval, allowing doily to show evenly around oval. Apply liquid ravel preventer at edges. Glue doily center on oval top as pictured. Glue oval, with raw edges at bottom, to center of lined basket. Cut white trim to fit around oval and glue.

5. Make petal pattern and transfer to remaining tablecloth fabric, positioning embroidered design in middle of each petal. Cut six. With wrong sides facing, stitch three petals, leaving an opening. Turn. Glue crochet trim to petals as desired.

6. Cut four 12" lengths of aqua ribbon. To make gathered bows, stitch gathering thread through center of 12" length. Pull thread tightly to gather and secure thread; see diagram.

Diagram

7. Glue one aqua bow to inside of basket at base of handle. Repeat, making three more aqua bows and one mauve bow. Glue bows and tablecloth petals to outside of basket at base of handle on opposite side; see photograph.

WAX SEALS

MATERIALS

Photograph on page 60.

Glass bottle of any shape
1½ yards of ⅞" ivory/gold
    wired ribbon
1¾ yards of 1½" ivory/gold
    wired ribbon
Gold metallic thread
Gold wax
Crest press

DIRECTIONS

1. Cut ⅞" ribbon to fit around bottle neck. Wrap ribbon around bottle, securing ends with glue.

2. Cut 2½" length of ⅞" ribbon. Drip hot wax onto center of ribbon, forming small, nickle-sized pool. Press crest in wax, making an imprint; lift crest. Let cool.

3. Cut 12" length of 1½" ribbon. Fold ribbon in half at angle to form upside-down V. Cut 9" length of ⅞" ribbon. Fold ribbon to form another upside-down V. Center and glue small V on top of larger one. Glue them both to ribbon around bottle neck. Cut small Vs at ribbon ends; see Diagram A.

4. Cut 10" length of 1½" ribbon. Fold ribbon in half to mark center. Fold ends together toward center, overlapping ¼". Sew gathering thread through center. Pull tightly to gather. Wrap thread around ribbon to secure. Repeat this step to make an additional bow. Make cross from two bows and glue centers together; see Diagram B.

Diagram B

Diagram A

5. Cut two 8" lengths of ⅞" ribbon. With two ribbons, make cross bow. Glue this bow to larger bow with loops spaced between each other; see Diagram C. Cut 2" length of 1½" ribbon. Fold edges over, overlapping in center. Glue small loop in center of bows covering gathering stitches.

Diagram C

6. With cooled ribbon seal, make circle, folding edges in toward center and over-lapping ¼". Glue ends together. Thread two 6" lengths of gold thread through center of seal circle. Press seal flat, letting it hang in center of thread; see Diagram D. Glue ends of thread to back of cross bow.

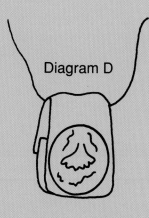

Diagram D

7. Glue cross bow to upside-down Vs.

8. Experiment with creative alternatives to sample. Here are some examples:

Option 1: Instead of cross bow used in sample, fold 12" length of ribbon in half. Stitch or glue short ends together. Sew gathering thread along edge of ribbon and pull thread tightly to gather. Place wax seal on ribbon and glue to center of gathered circle.

Option 2: On piece of stationery, label bottle in calligraphy or fancy writing; see pattern below. Rip edges of label to form an oval. To attach label to bottle body, position in place and drip hot wax along edges of oval. Attach ribbon to top of bottle neck with wax drippings. Wrap ribbon length of bottle at diagonal, attaching ends to bottle bottom and top. See photograph on page 40.

LABEL

SEWING BOX

MODEL

Photograph on page 66.

Stitched on moss green Morano 30 over two threads, finished design is 7⅛" x 1 ¾". Fabric was cut 16" x 12".

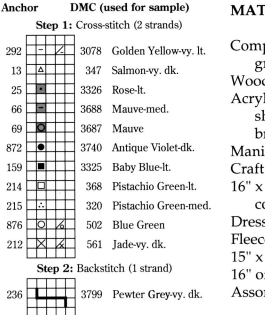

Anchor			DMC	(used for sample)
Step 1: Cross-stitch (2 strands)				
292	-	∕	3078	Golden Yellow-vy. lt.
13	△		347	Salmon-vy. dk.
25	▨		3326	Rose-lt.
66	▦		3688	Mauve-med.
69	◉		3687	Mauve
872	●		3740	Antique Violet-dk.
159	■		3325	Baby Blue-lt.
214	□		368	Pistachio Green-lt.
215	∴		320	Pistachio Green-med.
876	○	∕	502	Blue Green
212	✕	∕	561	Jade-vy. dk.
Step 2: Backstitch (1 strand)				
236	⌐		3799	Pewter Grey-vy. dk.

MATERIALS

Completed design on moss green Morano 30
Wood sewing box
Acrylic paints: three green shades, pink, red, orange, brown
Manila folder
Craft knife
16" x 12" piece of fabric; contrasting thread
Dressmaker's pen
Fleece
15" x 11" piece of cardboard
16" of ½" ivory lace
Assorted buttons

STITCH COUNT 107 X 26

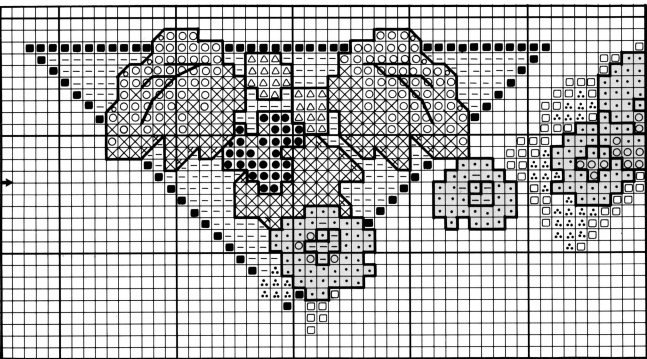

DIRECTIONS

1. Paint sewing box green. Let paint dry. With red paint, paint edges of handle and along top edge of box sides. Let paint dry.

2. Trace patterns on page 67. Using scrap of carbon paper, transfer berry pattern to top of box, placing three on each side. Repeat with flower pattern, placing three on each side of box; see photograph. Paint as desired. Let paint dry.

3. Using dressmaker's pen, mark quilting lines on right side of fabric as shown on pattern; see page 67. Cut 15½" x 11½" piece of fleece and sandwich it between wrong sides of fabric and design piece; baste. Machine quilt through all layers with contrasting thread. Attach lace ½" above finished design piece. Stitch buttons as shown on pattern.

4. Center cardboard on wrong side of design piece. Wrap edges of fabric around cardboard back and secure with glue. Glue quilted design piece to front of box.

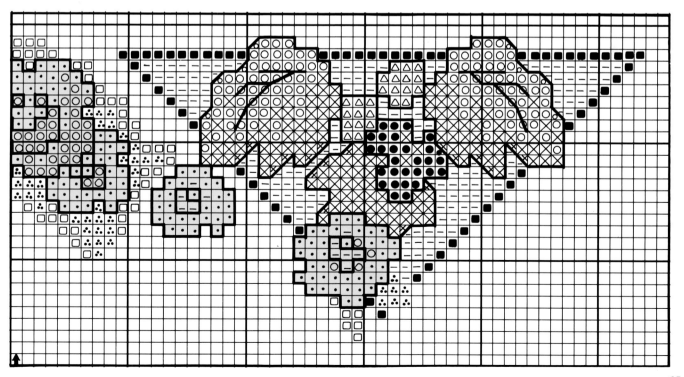

BERRY

FLOWER

1 SQUARE = 1 INCH

*Welcome family and friends into a warm
home full of gifts made especially with each
person in mind. For a dear friend, stitch a ribbon-
adorned photo frame. For a daughter, let a wistful
angel light up her room. For a son, quilt some
pieced stockings to hold Christmas goodies.
For a father, paint goblets and needlepoint
coasters. For a mother, crochet a delicate mirror
and hat box. For an egg-centric aunt, cover an
egg form with cloth, ribbons and beads.
And suprise a granddaughter with a
a handkerchief doll and a ribbon stocking
for her first Christmas.*

FOR OUR DEAR FRIEND

PHOTO FRAME

MATERIALS

Photograph on page 68.

10" square of cardboard
10" square of mauve satin
    fabric
6" square of peach satin fabric
6" square of polyester fleece
Tacky glue
7" length of gold metallic
    cording
Hot glue gun and glue sticks
½ yard of ¾" multicolored
    wired ribbon
¾ yard of ¼" rose silk ribbon
5" length of ⅛" purple silk
    ribbon
Dressmaker's pen
Needle and thread
Silk embroidery thread: two
    rose shades, one leaf
    shade
¾ yard of ⅛" lavender silk
    ribbon
¾ yard of ⅛" burgundy silk
    ribbon
Fifteen pastel seed beads
12" length of ¼" olive trim
¼ yard of ¼" tatting or lace

DIRECTIONS

See General Instructions to embroider bullion roses, to cascade ribbon and to make ribbon rosettes and French knots.

1. Make frame patterns and transfer to cardboard. Cut two front and two back pieces. From fleece, cut one frame front. Glue fleece to one cardboard frame front.

2. Add ½" around frame front pattern and cut two from mauve fabric. Add ½" around frame back pattern; cut one from mauve fabric and one from peach fabric.

3. Place cardboard frame front, fleece side down, centered on wrong side of mauve fabric front piece. Wrap and glue fabric edges to back, clipping curves. Redefine scallops and curves using fingernail and extra glue. Gently press with warm iron to smooth puckers. Repeat with second cardboard frame front and mauve fabric front piece. Repeat with cardboard back and mauve fabric pieces, then cardboard back and peach fabric pieces.

4. Fold gold cording in half; tie knot at looped end ¾" down. Using hot glue, attach cording ends to wrong side of mauve frame back . Position ends ½" apart and ¼" down from top of frame back so that loop is centered at top for hanger. Using ½ yard multicolored wired ribbon, make ribbon rosette. Glue rosette to loop knot on hanger.

5. To flute frame back, glue end of rose silk ribbon at angle on wrong side of mauve frame back. Starting at bottom center, fold ribbon back and forth diagonally, extending ribbon loops ¼" beyond frame edge. Lining up edges, glue wrong side of peach frame back to wrong side mauve frame back, covering raw fabric and inside fluting edges. Set aside.

6. Set aside frame front piece without fleece. With purple silk ribbon, make small ribbon rosette. Using dressmaker's pen, mark on front/fleece piece center top for rosette placement. Also mark placement of embroidered bullion roses and ribbon French knots; see photograph. Stitch rosette in place.

7. Using embroidery thread, stitch bullion roses, alternating colors on petals.

Using lazy-daisy stitch, scatter leaves around roses. Thread embroidery needles with lavender silk ribbon. Stitch nineteen French knots around bottom half of oval opening.

8. Secure burgundy ribbon on wrong side of frame front centered at bottom and pull ribbon ends through to front.

Tie small bow. Secure bow. Thread embroidery needle with bow ends and cascade ribbon up each side, twisting between stitches to give more curl; see photograph for placement. Stitch seed beads along cascading ribbon ends and around frame front as desired.

9. Glue edge of olive trim underneath outer edge of frame front. Glue tatting underneath inner edge of frame front. Glue frame front to remaining frame front piece with wrong sides facing, covering raw fabric edges. Glue completed frame back to completed front, leaving top third open for picture insert.

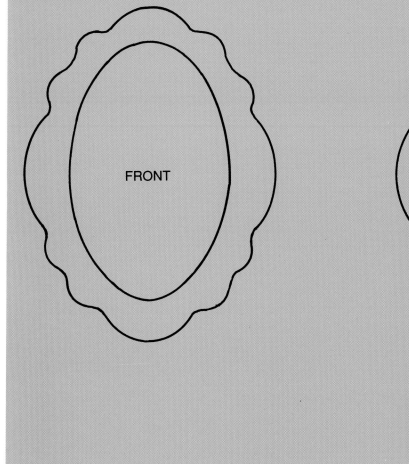

FRONT

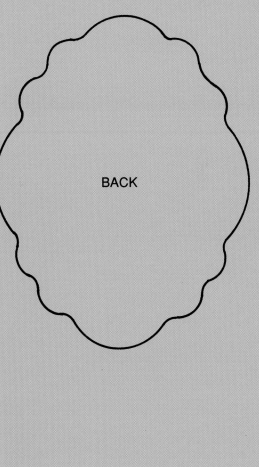

BACK

FOR OUR DAUGHTER

PORCELAIN DOLL

MATERIALS

10"-tall porcelain doll
1 yard of patterned tulle
 fabric; matching thread
½ yard of cream fabric
¼ yard of cream bridal tulle
 fabric
2 yards of 2"-wide cream lace
2 yards of 1½"-wide cream
 lace trim
Craft wire
Iridescent confetti
Iridescent seed beads
Transparent thread
1 yard of ½"-wide cream satin
 ribbon
Snaps

DIRECTIONS

All seams are ¼" unless
otherwise indicated.

1. Trace patterns on page 75.
From patterned tulle fabric,
cut one bodice front, two
bodice backs and two sleeves.
Also cut one 9" x 36" skirt
piece, one 3" x 45" piece for
puff border, and one ¾" x 8"
for neck ruffle.

2. From cream fabric, cut two
bodice fronts, four bodice
backs, two sleeves and one 9"
x 28" skirt strip. From cream
tulle, cut two 8"-wide circles
and two 10"-wide circles for
wings.

3. Cut 3½" length of 2"-wide
cream lace. Center over tulle
bodice; baste. Place lining
front and back bodice right
side over tulle bodice. With
right sides of tulle bodice
facing, align edges. Stitch
shoulders, open. Repeat for
other lining front and back;
open.

4. For ruffle, fold ¾" x 8" strip
of tulle in half lengthwise. Sew
gathering stitch along raw
edge; pull thread to gather.
Sandwich ruffle around
neckline between tulle and
lining. With right sides of tulle
bodice and lining facing right
sides of other lining, stitch

along one center back seam,
around neck and down
second center back seam. Clip
curved edges.

5. Fold sleeve lining and tulle
under ⅛" along straight edge,
zigzag stitch and gather to 6"
length to form cuff. Zigzag
stitch 4" length of elastic ½"
above cuff. Run gathering
stitch along sleeve cap; gather
sleeve to fit armhole. With right
sides facing, stitch sleeve to
bodice. Turn sleeve. With right
sides facing, stitch bodice side
seam and sleeve seam. Repeat
with remaining sleeve.

6. For skirt, fold lining ⅛"
along long edge, zigzag stitch
and gather, pulling to 26"
length. On top edge of lining,
sew gathering thread. On tulle
skirt piece, with right sides
facing and edges aligned, sew
gathered length of lace to
bottom edge. On top edge of
tulle skirt piece, sew gathering
thread. Gather top edges of
two skirt pieces to fit bodice
opening. With center seam
opening on back of bodice
skirt aligned, and right sides
facing, sew skirt pieces to
bodice. Sew center back seam
of skirt lining to within 2" of
bodice seam; backstitch.
Repeat with tulle skirt piece.

7. For wings, bend four lengths of wire into mushroom shapes in desired size. Allow 2" of wire ends at stem for attaching; see Diagram A. Place wire on plain tulle circles, pile iridescent confetti in center and wrap tulle around wire wings, securing tulle at bottom. With transparent thread, attach tulle to wire with slipstiches of beads around edge of wing; after each stitch, thread twelve beads. Backstitch entire wing forming crossing slipstitches with beads. Repeat with three remaining wings.

Diagram A

8. Bring ends of wings together with large wings above small ones; see Diagram B. Wrap wires with remaining tulle; secure with thread. Tack wings to center back of bodice. Sew two snaps on top and bottom center back of bodice.

Diagram B

9. Fold 3"-wide tulle in half lengthwise. With wrong sides facing, stitch long edges. Loosely tack seam of tulle, centered lengthwise, to 2 yards of 1½"-wide cream lace trim. Fold this strip in half lengthwise with right sides facing. Matching fold to bottom seam of tulle skirt piece, tack strip to skirt. Stitch three rows of seed beads around tulle strip every 2" to make puffs; see Diagram C.

Diagram C

10. Cut satin ribbon to 27" length; cut Vs at ends. At center of ribbon, loop five seed beads and attach. Repeat, looping seed beads 1" apart on both sides of center, making five stitches total. Wrap ribbon around waist of angel; tie bow in back.

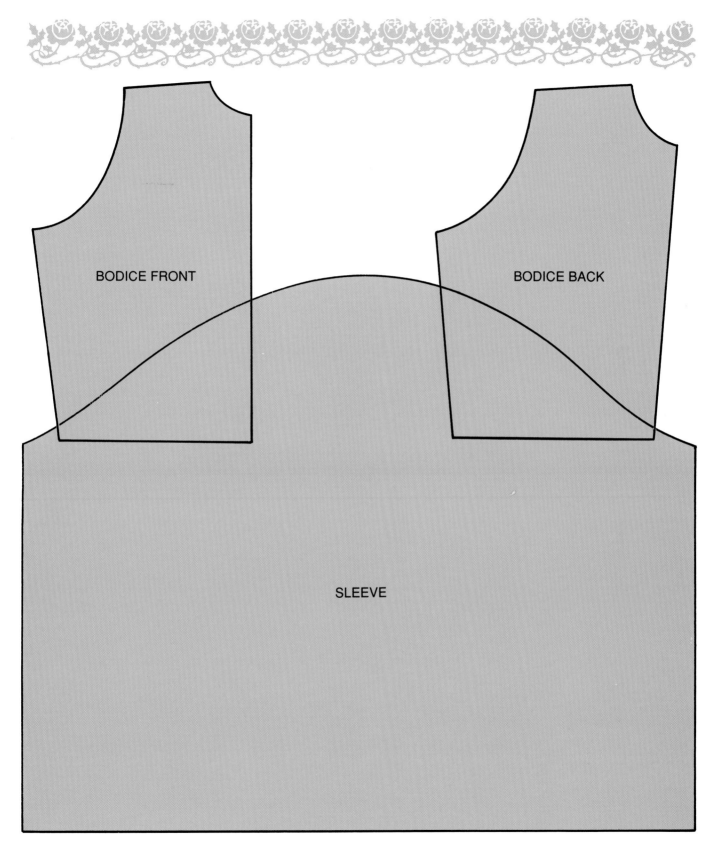

BODICE FRONT

BODICE BACK

SLEEVE

FOR OUR SON

QUILTED STOCKINGS

MATERIALS (for one)

⅝ yard of print fabric for
    stocking back; matching
    thread
⅝ yard of print fabric for
    stocking lining; matching
    thread
⅝ yard of muslin
⅝ yard of polyester fleece
Red and green print fabric
    scraps
Assorted buttons, trim,
    ribbon, embroidery floss
    and ornaments
Package of purchased muslin
    corded piping
6" length of ¼" grosgrain
    ribbon

DIRECTIONS

1. Make stocking pattern on page 78. Cut two stockings from lining fabric, one from backing fabric, one from muslin and two from fleece. On right side of muslin, mark heel and toe. Cut heel and toe from pattern. From scrap fabrics, cut one heel and one toe, adding seam allowances to inside edges.

2. Cut some scrap fabric into 1", 1 ¼" and 1 ½"-wide strips for crazy quilting. Also, separate any decorative motifs which might be appliquéd on surface. Layer muslin, fleece and one wide strip, right side up, across top of stocking. Continue to add scraps at odd angles, placing second piece over fruit and stitching through all layers. Unfold second piece and repeat, adding third and so on. Some seams may need to be done by hand. Add heel and toe last. Embellish some seams with embroidery stitches, appliqué decorative motifs, and sew on buttons and trim as desired. Trim crazy-quilt surface to match muslin.

3. Pin second fleece stocking to wrong side of stocking back. Stitch crazy-quilt stocking front to back, right sides facing, and leaving top edge open. Trim fleece from seam allowance. Turn. Stitch corded piping to top edge edge on right side. Fold 6" grosgrain ribbon in half. Pin ends to upper edge of stocking back near seam above heel.

4. Stitch lining pieces together with right sides facing, leaving top edge open and an opening in seam above heel; do not turn. Slide lining over stocking, matching side seams. Stitch around top on stitching line of piping. Turn through opening in side seam. Slipstitch opening closed. Fold lining inside stocking.

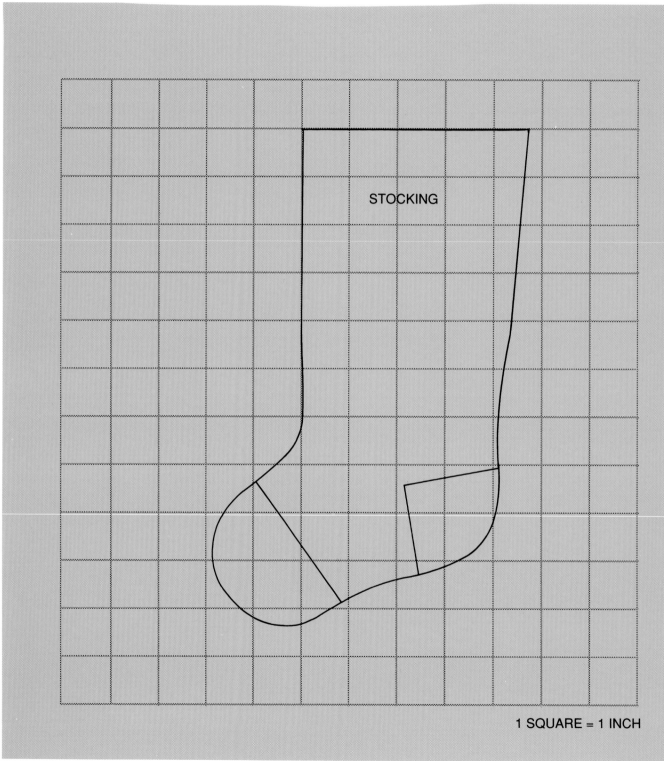

STOCKING

1 SQUARE = 1 INCH

FOR OUR FATHER

PAINTED GOBLETS

MATERIALS

Photograph on page 80.

Two 5½"-tall glass goblets
Gloss enamel paint: red, blue,
   yellow, green, brown
Paintbrush

DIRECTIONS

1. Make fish patterns. Leaving border around pattern, cut each one. Position and tape individual patterns to inside of one goblet.

2. Paint fish as desired; see photograph. Let paint dry.

3. Beginning at bottom of glass stem, paint one blue horizontal stripe around stem. About ½" above blue stripe, paint one red horizontal stripe around stem. Paint yellow dots above red stripe; see photograph.

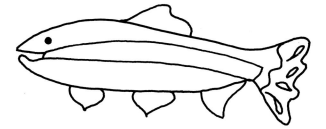

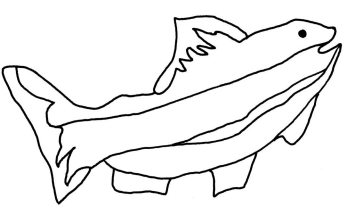

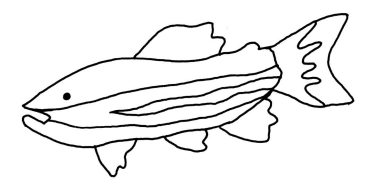

FISH PATTERNS

NEEDLEPOINT COASTERS

MODEL

Graph on page 82.

Stitched on Needlepoint Canvas 14, the finished design size for both coasters is 4¼" x 4¼". The canvas was cut 8" x 8" for each.

Paternayan Persian yarn (used for sample)

Step 1: Continental stitch (1 ply)

⊙				733	Honey Gold
·				484	Terra Cotta
✕				900	American Beauty
●				500	Federal Blue
◎				691	Loden Green
▲				452	Khaki Brown
−				900	American Beauty
				or	
				500	Federal Blue

MATERIALS (for two coasters)

Photograph on page 80.

Completed designs on Needlepoint Canvas 14; matching thread
10" square of fleece
10" square of upholstery velvet

DIRECTIONS

1. With design centered, trim design pieces to 5" square. From fleece, cut two 5" squares. From upholstery velvet, cut two 5" squares.

2. With right sides facing and edges aligned, layer one fleece piece, one design piece (right side up) and one piece of velvet (wrong side up). Stitch together with ½" seam, rounding corners and leaving an opening. Clip corners; turn so that fleece is sandwiched between design and velvet. Slipstitch opening closed. Repeat for second coaster.

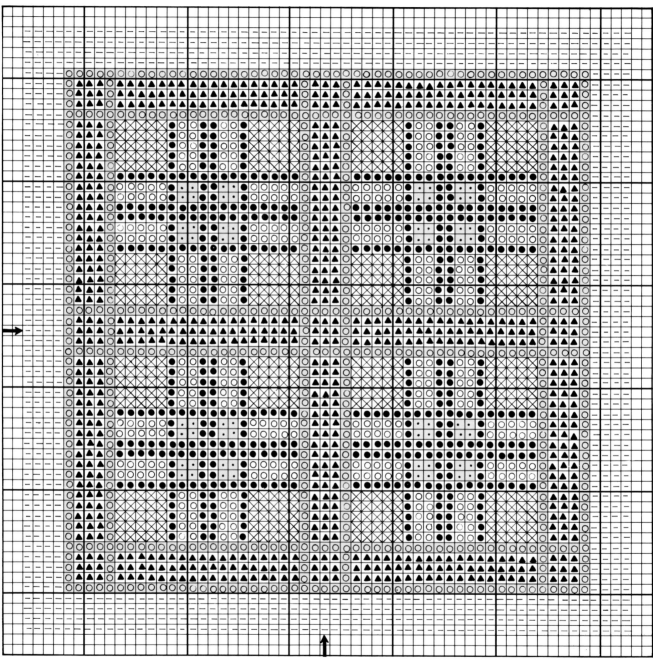

STITCH COUNT: 59 x 59

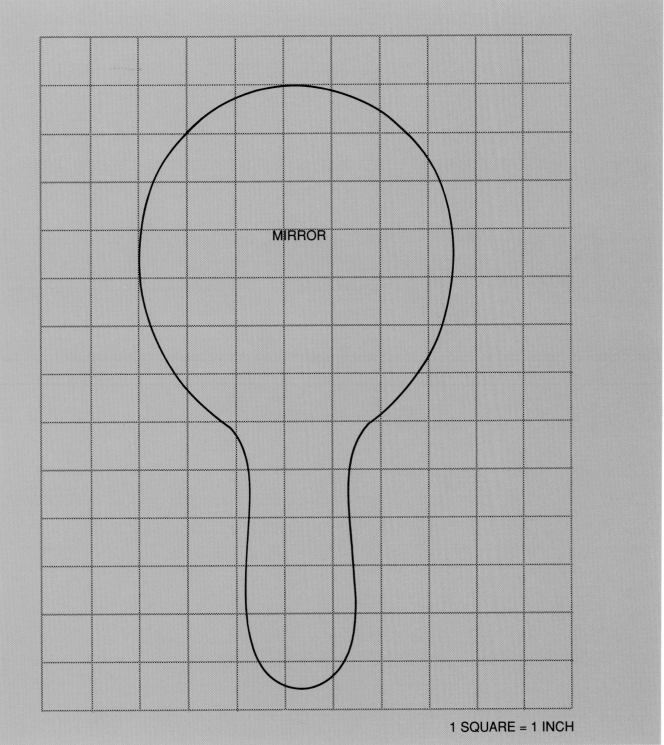

MIRROR

1 SQUARE = 1 INCH

HAT BOX & MIRROR

MATERIALS (for hat box)

Round cardboard hat box,
    14" wide x 4¼" deep
1½ yards of green fabric
4 yards of green 2"-wide
    wired ribbon
3 yards of ivory 1½"-wide
    wired ribbon
3 yards of crochet trim
40" length of ¾" cording
Tacky glue

DIRECTIONS

*See General Instructions to make
ribbon flowers, leaves and petals.*

1. From fleece, cut two pieces
to fit top of lid. Cut green
fabric to fit top of lid, adding
½" all around. From green
fabric, cut 2" x 46" strip and
5½" x 46" strip. Also cut circle
to fit box bottom less ¼"
around.

2. Glue two layers of fleece to
top of lid. Place lid fleece side
down on wrong side of green
fabric. Wrap fabric around top
of lid and glue edges to sides
of lid. Glue 2"-wide fabric
strip around side of lid with
raw edge along top edge. Turn
remaining fabric under lid and
glue. Glue crochet border
around lid, covering fabric
raw edge.

3. Glue 5½"-wide fabric strip
around box bottom, tucking
and gluing ¼" to box bottom.
Glue 13½" circle to bottom of
box, covering raw edges of
fabric strip. Glue crochet
border around box 1½" from
bottom.

4. Poke two holes in side of
box across from each other.
Thread cording through sides,
tying cording in knot on
inside of box to secure.

5. From ivory ribbon, cut
seven 12" lengths for large
flowers and four 6" lengths for
small flowers. From green
ribbon, cut eight 12" lengths
for large flowers, two 6"
lengths for small leaves, and
eighteen 2" lengths for ribbon
petals. Make flowers, leaves
and petals. Arrange as desired
on top of box lid; glue in place.

MATERIALS (for mirror)

10" x 15" piece of ¼"-thick
    plywood
Jigsaw
Two crocheted mirror pieces
1½ yards of green fabric;
    matching thread
1½ yards of fleece
6½" x 5½" oval mirror

DIRECTIONS

1. Make mirror frame pattern
on page 83 and cut one from
plywood.

2. To make fabric pattern,
trace around mirror frame,
adding ½" all around. Cut
two from green fabric. From
fleece, cut two mirror pieces
and two head pieces without
handles. Trim ⅛" all around
one fleece head piece. Trim
¼" from other head piece.

3. On mirror back, center and
layer fleece mirror pieces on
top of one another. Begin by
gluing smallest fleece head to
mirror back, then glue larger
head on top of it, then glue
entire fleece piece on top of
smaller pieces. Glue remaining fleece piece on other side.

4. With right sides together,
stitch green fabric pieces
together, leaving opening at
top. Turn. Slip over mirror.
Turn seam allowance under
and slipstitch opening closed.

5. Center and glue oval mirror
to front, lightly padded side.
Stitch inside edge of crochet
edging around mirror and
outside edge around frame.
Stitch crochet handle piece to
handle at edges. On back of
mirror, stitch crochet back
piece around outside edges.

FINISHED SIZE

Mirror cover approximately 7" x 8" plus handle 2" x 5", hat box approximately 14" diameter x 4⅝" high (approximately 44" around).

MATERIALS (for crochet)

Yarn description: Crochet cotton #20, Tan

Yarn pictured: Schewe Fil D'Ecosse #16, 50-gr., 400 m balls, 1 ball Tan #164

Tools: Size 7 steel hook.

GAUGE
1 outer scallop = 1½".

DIRECTIONS

5 dc pc = Make 5 dc, remove hook from lp, insert hook in top of first dc, pick up dropped lp, pull lp through. Note: If pc is not followed by chs, ch 1 to close.
Ch link = ch 4, dc in 3rd ch from hook, (ch 3, dc bet dc and ch 3).

Bottom trim:
Rnd 1: Make 132 ch links, do not twist, join with sl st in beg link to form a ring, sl st in next ch of same link for base rnd.
Rnd 2: Work down ch side of link, sc in same link * ch 4, dc in 4th ch from hook, make 6 more ch links, make ea one as follows: ch 3, dc bet prev ch

and dc, sk 5 links of base rnd, * * sc in next link (7 ch link lp), rep from * around, except end last rep at * *, sl st to beg sc = 22 lps.
Rnd 3: Sl st in next link, ch 5, [* (dc, ch 2, dc) in next link, ch 2, rep from * 4 times, dec as follows over next 2 links: yo, insert hook in next link, pull up a lp, yo, pull through 2 lps on hook, yo, insert hook in next link, pull up a lp, yo, pull through 2 lps on hook, yo, pull through rem 3 lps on hook, ch 2], rep bet [ ] around, end last rep at * *, insert hook in 3rd ch of beg ch-5, pull thread through, yo, pull through rem 3 lps.
Rnd 4: [Sc in next sp, * (sc, ch 3, 5-dc pc, ch 4, sc) in next sp, (sc, ch 3, sc) in next sp, rep from * 3 times, (sc, ch 3, pc, ch 4, sc) in next sp, sc in next sp], rep bet [ ] around, sl st to beg sc. Fasten off.

Top trim edge: Rep rnds 1-4.

Top popcorn edge: Join to base rnd in center of any link, ch 4, 4 dc in same link, drop lp from hook, insert hook in top of ch-4, pull dropped lp through, ch 1 to close, (2 5-dc pcs in next link, * popcorn in next link) around end last rep at *, sl st to top of beg ch-4. Fasten off.

Mirror cover back section:
With A, ch 8, sl st to beg ch to form a ring.

Rnd 1: Ch 1, 18 sc in ring, sl st to beg sc =18 sc.
Rnd 2: Ch 4, sk 1 st, * (5-dc popcorn, sh 1, 5-dc popcorn) in next st, ch 2, * * hdc in next st, ch 2, sk 1 st, rep from * around, end last rep at * *, sl st to 2nd ch of beg ch-4 =6 double popcorn grps.
Rnd 3: Ch 6, (sc in ch-1 sp bet next 2 popcorns, ch 5 sc in next hdc, ch 5) around, sc to beg ch =12 lps.
Rnd 4: *(Ch 5, sc in next 1p) twice, ch 5, sc in next sc, rep from * around = 18 lps.
Rnd 5: * (Ch 6, sc in next 1p) 3 times, ch 6, sc in next sc, rep from * around = 24 lps.
Rnd 6: * 2 sc in next lp, (ch 6, sc in next lp) twice, ch 6, 2 sc in next lp, rep from * around, sl st to beg sc.
Rnd 7: Ch 3, popcorn in same st, *ch 3, sc in next lp, (ch 7 sc in next lp) twice, ch 3, * * poopcorn bet 2nd and 3rd sc, rep from *around, end last rep at * *, sl st to top of beg ch-3.
Rnd 8: Sc in same st, * (ch 8, sc in next lp) twice, ch 8, * * sc in top of next popcorn, rep from * around, end last rep at * *, sl st to beg sc.
Rnd 9: (Sc, ch 3, sc, ch 3, sc, ch 3, sc) in next lp around, sl st to beg sc.
Rnd 10: Ch 3, (popcorn, ch 3, popcorn) in same st, * ch 12, sk 4 ch-3 lps, sc in next lp, ch 12, sk 4 ch-3 lps, * * (popcorn, ch 3, popcorn) bet next 2 sc, rep from * around, end last rep at

* *, sl st to top of beg ch-3.

Rnd 11: Sc in ch-1 closure of next popcorn, (ch 12, sc in next popcorn, ch 9, sc in next lp, ch 12, sc in next lp, ch 9, sc in next popcorn) around, sl st to beg sc, sl st in ea of next 6 ch.

Fnd 12: Sc in same lp, (ch 8, * sc in next lp) around, end last rep at *, sl st to beg sc.

Rnd 13: * (Sc, ch 5, sc, sh 5, sc, sh 5, sc) in next lp, rep from * around, sl st to beg sc.

Rnd 14: * Ch 4, dc in 4th ch from hook, make 6 more ch links, make ea one as follows: ch3, dc bet prev ch and dc, sk 6 lps, sc bet next 2 sc = 7 ch link lps, rep from * around = 12 lps, sl st in next st.

Rnd 15: Ch 5, [* (dc, ch 2, dc) in next link, ch 2, rep from *4 times, dec as follows over next 2 links: yo, insert hook in next link, pull up a lp, yo, pull through 2 lps on hook, * * yo, pull through rem 3 lps on hook, ch 2], rep bet [ ] around, end last rep at * *, insert hook in 3rd ch of beg ch-5, pull up a lps, yo pull through rem 3 lps.

Rnd 16: [Sc in next sp, * (sc, ch 3, 5-dc popcorn, ch 4, sc) in next sp, (sc, ch 3, sc) in next sp, rep from * 3 times, (sc, ch 3, popcorn, ch 4, sc) in next sp, sc in next sp], rep bet [ ] around, sl st to beg sc, Fasten off.

Mirror cover/Handle cover:

Row 1: Join A to top of center popcorn of last link lp worked with sc, ch 3, dc in 3rd ch from hook, make 6 more ch links as in rnd 14, sk 4 popcorn, sc in next popcorn, turn.

Row 2: Push popcorn to right side of work, ch 3, popcorn in sc just made, *ch, [dc, ch 2, dc (v-st)] in next link, rep from *6 times, ch 2, popcorn in next sc, dc in same sc, turn.

Row 3: (Ch 5, sc in center ch-2 of next v st) 7 times, ch 2, dc in top of beg ch-3 at end of prev row, turn.

Row 4: (Ch 5, sc in next lp) 6 times, ch 2, dc in next lp, turn.

Row 5: Ch 3, popcorn in same dc, make 3 links as in row 1, sk next 2 lps, (popcorn, ch 3, popcorn) in next lp, make 3 links, sk next 2 lps, popcorn in center ch of next lp, make 3 links, sk next 2 lps, popcorn in center ch of next lp, dc in same st, turn.

Row 6: (Ch 5, sc in next link)3 times, ch 5, sc in ch-3 lp bet popcorns, (ch 5, sc in next link) 3 times, ch 2, dc in top of beg ch-3 of prev row, turn.

Row 7: (Ch 5, sc in next lp) 6 times, ch 2, dc in center ch of next lp, turn.

Row 8: (Ch 5, sc in next lp) 5 times, ch 2, dc in center ch of next lp, turn.

Row 9: Ch 3, popcorn in same dc, make 3 links, sk 1 lp, (popcorn, ch 3, popcorn) in ea of next 2 lps, make 3 links, sk 1 lp, popcorn in center ch of next lp, dc in same st, turn.

Row 10: (Ch 5, sc in next link) 3 times, ch 5, sc bet next 2 popcorn grps, rep bet ( ) 3 times, ch 3, dc in top of beg ch-3, turn.

Row 11: (Ch 5, sc in next lp) 6 times, ch 2, dc in center ch of next lp, turn.

Row 12: Rep row 8.

Rows 13-16: Rep rows 9-12.

Row 17: (Ch 5, sc in next lp) 4 times, ch 2, dc in center ch of next lp, turn.

Rows 18-21: Rep row 17, except rep bet ( ) one less time in ea row. Fasten off at end of row 19.

Front section:

Rd 1: Make 60 ch links, take care not to twist sl st in center of beg link to form a ring, sl st in next ch of same link.

Rnd 2: Work down ch side of link, sc in same link, rep rnd 2 of hat box trim, except sk only 4 links instead of 5 = 12 lps of 7 links ea.

Rnd 3: Rep rnd 3 of hat box trim.

Rnd 4: Rep rnd 4 of hat box trim.

Rep handle cover. Fasten off.

FOR OUR EGG-CENTRIC AUNT

RIBBON EGG

This ornament can be mounted on an antique frame hanger as pictured. Replace cording hanger with brass hanger on wooden frame. Cut chain to proper length so ornament is suspended.

MATERIALS

4" plastic craft egg
6" x 12" piece of fleece
6" x 12" piece of pink satin
Six 2½" fabric circles in
    assorted colors
¼ yard each of ¼" silk ribbon:
    six pastel shades
10" each of ⅛" ribbon: nine
    pastel shades
½ yard of ⅛" pink silk ribbon
Silk embroidery thread: five
    pink shades, two green
    shades
12" length of 1" multicolored
    wired ribbon
9" length of ½" multicolored
    wired ribbon
Thirty assorted seed beads
    and small pearls
Six rhinestones
Three small brass charms
Tacky glue

DIRECTIONS

See General Instructions to embroider bullion rosettes, to cascade ribbon and to make yo-yos, ribbon rosettes and leaves.

1. Glue plastic egg halves together. Glue fleece to egg as smoothly as possible. Trim.

2. Fold satin in half, with right sides facing and short edges aligned, stitching ¼" seam. Press seam open. Turn and slip fabric tube over egg. Fold top edge down ¼" and stitch gathering thread around edge; see diagram. Pull thread tightly to gather and secure. Glue gathered satin to egg. Repeat on bottom edge of egg.

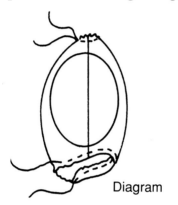
Diagram

3. Make six yo-yos with 2½" fabric circles. Cut ¼" silk ribbon into six 9" lengths and make six rosettes. Cut ⅛" silk ribbon into eighteen 5" lengths and make eighteen rosettes.

4. To place embroidered bullion petals, measure 1½" from top of egg. Lightly mark seven places at equal distance from each other around egg. Stitch bullion petals, alternating stitches with different shades of thread. With green silk embroidery thread, embroider leaves using lazy-daisy stitch. Thread

needle with ½ yard of pink silk ribbon and cascade around bullions, twisting ribbon to give more curl. Stitch beads and pearls around roses; see photograph.

5. For placement of larger rosettes, measure 2½" from top center of egg. Lightly mark six places an equal distance from each other around egg. Glue rosettes in place. Glue three ⅛" rosettes, alternating colors, in an arch between larger rosettes. Glue yo-yos below arch. Glue rhinestones in yo-yo centers. For hanger, loop 7" length of cording, knotting ends. Glue knot to center top of egg.

6. To make ribbon ruffles, fold 12" length of 1" wired ribbon with right sides facing and short edges aligned; glue or stitch small seam. Turn. Stitch gathering thread around one long edge of ribbon. Pull thread tightly to gather, leaving small center opening. Place ruffled ribbon circle on top of egg, carefully threading hanger through center opening. Glue to egg without matting ruffles. Repeat, using 9" length of ½" wired ribbon.

7. Bend charms slightly so they are flat against curved surface of egg; glue.

FOR OUR GRANDDAUGHTER

HANDKERCHIEF DOLL

MATERIALS

Five 7"-square white
    handkerchiefs; matching
    thread
1½ yards of 1½" scalloped lace
4¼ yards of ¹⁄₁₆" pink braid
Polyester stuffing
Acrylic paints: peach, pink,
    red, blue, black, white
Nylon thread

DIRECTIONS

All seams are ⅛".

1. Set aside one handkerchief for blanket. Make and transfer patterns on page 92 to remaining handkerchiefs. Cut two bodies, two gowns and one 3¼" x 1¼" piece for bonnet.

2. To make baby, stitch body pieces together with right sides facing, leaving an opening on one side. Clip inside corners. Turn. Stuff firmly. Slipstitch opening closed. Wrap double strand of thread around neck and pull tightly; secure threads. Paint face; see Diagram A.

Diagram A

3. To make gown, zigzag raw edges of neck and wrists. With right sides facing, stitch gown pieces together along right and left edges and shoulders, leaving neck and wrists open.

4. Fold zigzagged edges of neck under; stitch. Cut one 24" braid and two 4" lengths of braid. With 24" braid, stitch gathering threads along folded edge of neck. Repeat at wrists of sleeves using 4" braids and leaving ends free; do not cut.

5. Stitch ⅛" hem on bottom edge of gown. Cut one 8" length of lace. With right sides facing, fold lace in half and stitch short edges together. With seam in back, place lace right side up over right side of hem on gown. Stitch top edge of lace ¼" above hem.

6. Cut one 16" length of braid. With braid, begin at center front of gown and hand stitch gathering thread through straight edge of lace at hem. Tie ends in bow at center front. Place gown on doll. Pull braid at neck to gather, tie in bow at front leaving long tails. Gather sleeve braids and tie in bows.

7. To make bonnet, cut 3½" length of lace. Position lace over bonnet piece with right sides facing (lace will extend beyond front edge). Stitch sides and back, leaving front edge open. Turn. Fold front edge of bonnet fabric under; slipstitch closed. Stitch gathering thread along back edge of bonnet and gather to fit neck of doll. Secure threads. Cut one 21" length of braid. With braid, stitch gathering thread along front of bonnet ¼" from edge, leaving 9" tails. Tie bonnet in place with bow at chin.

8. To make blanket, cut four 10" lengths of lace. Place lace lengths right side up and ¼" over right edges of handkerchief. Stitch, mitering corners; see Diagram B. Cut one 40" length of braid. Thread through inside lace edge. Tie ends in bow at one corner.

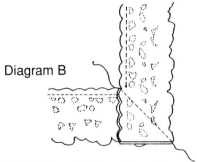

Diagram B

9. Cut two 20" lengths of braid. Wrap blanket around doll, double tie braids in bow at waist. For hanger, make loop with nylon thread; attach where desired.

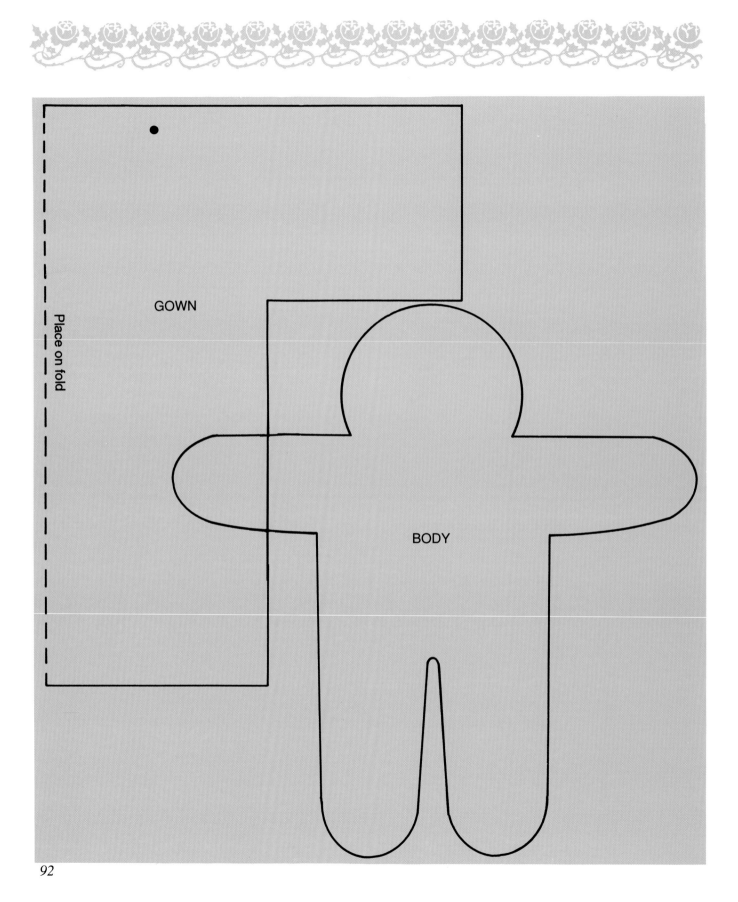

GOWN

Place on fold

BODY

92

RIBBON STOCKING

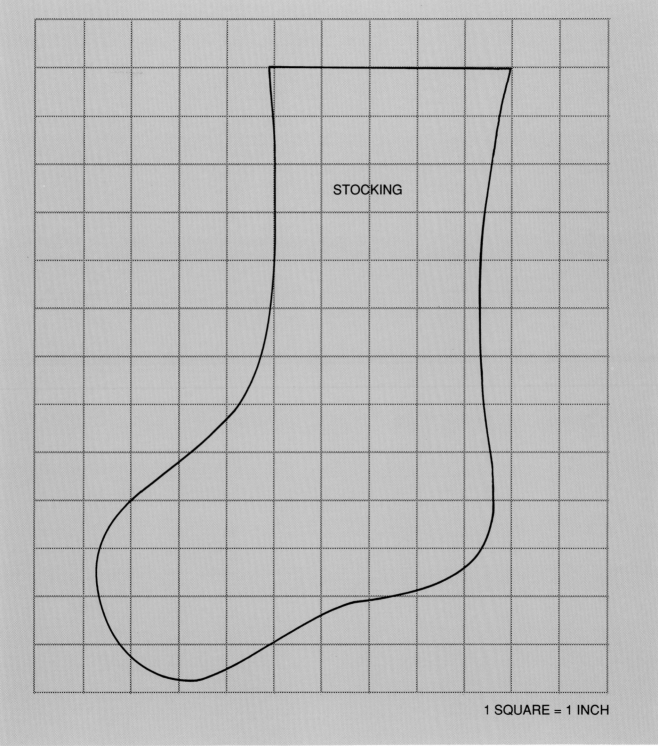

STOCKING

1 SQUARE = 1 INCH

RIBBON STOCKING

MATERIALS

1 yard of white fabric;
   matching thread
White pillowcase with
   embroidered edge
1 yard of ⅛" white corded
   piping
8 yards each of blue, yellow
   and pink ⅛" silk ribbon
3 yards of green ⅛" silk ribbon
12" length of 1"-wide pink lace
7" length of white ¼" silk
   ribbon
Seed beads, pearl beads and
   crystal beads
Hot glue gun and glue

DIRECTIONS
All seams are ⅛".

*See General Instructions to make
ribbon rosettes and leaves.*

1. Make pattern on page 93 for
stocking. From white fabric,
cut two stocking and two
lining pieces.

2. For ribbon rosettes, cut blue,
yellow and pink silk ribbon
into 12" lengths. Make twenty-
two blue rosettes, twenty-two
yellow rosettes and twenty-
seven pink rosettes.

3. For ribbon leaves, cut green
silk ribbon into 2" lengths.
Make fifty-two ribbon leaves.

4. On embroidered pillowcase
scrap, embellish the existing
design with groups of ribbon
roses. Arrange and attach seed
beads and pearls as desired;
see photograph.

5. Pin pillowcase piece right
side up on top edge of stocking
front. Trim pillowcases to
match stockings. With right
sides of piping and stocking
front facing and raw edges
aligned, stitch piping around
sides and bottom of stocking.
With right sides facing and raw
edges aligned, stitch stocking
front to stocking back, sewing
on stitching line of piping and
leaving top edges open. Clip
curves. Turn. Gather and baste
12" length of 1"-wide pink lace
to seam along top edge of
stocking.

6. To make stocking lining,
with right sides facing and raw
edges aligned, stitch together
lining front and back, leaving
top edge open and large
opening in side seam above
heel. Clip curves. Do not turn.
With right sides facing, slide
lining over stocking, matching
side seams. Cut 6" length of
white silk ribbon for hanger.
Fold ribbon in half with wrong

sides facing. Sandwich hanger
between lining and stocking
top. With raw edges aligned,
stitch lining to stocking top,
securing hanger and lace in
seam. Turn stocking through
opening in lining. Slipstitch
opening closed. Tuck lining
inside stocking.

7. On finished edge of
pillowcase piece, glue six
groups of three roses and two
green leaves. Space groupings
½" apart along finished edge
of pillowcase piece. Attach
strand of seed beads to
pillowcase. Starting at first
rose group, loop sixteen beads
and attach at second rose
group. Loop sixteen more
beads and attach at third
group. Loop twenty-one seed
beads, then large crystal bead,
then twenty-one more seed
beads; attach at forth rose
group. Attach sixteen seed
bead loops to remaining rose
groups. On stocking front,
arrange roses and leaves to
form stocking toe and heel.
With about eight roses each
color for heel and eight for toe,
glue roses to stocking;
alternate colors and insert
leaves between every three;
see photograph.

Romance and gift-giving seem to go hand-in-hand. For the lover of sweets, give hand-painted rose cookies. For the adventurer, map the way with a compass box. For the designer, stitch together fruit-shaped pincushions in a crochet basket. For the lover of books, offer frilly basket bookends. For the lover of tea parties, bundle an old tea set in moss.

For The Romantic

CHAPTER
5

ROSE COOKIES

MATERIALS

Photograph on page 96.

Cookie Dough:
½ cup butter or margarine, softened
½ cup shortening
1 cup sifted powdered sugar
1 egg
1½ to 2 teaspoons lemon extract
2½ cups all-purpose flour
½ teaspoon salt

Edible Decorator Paint:
1 egg yolk
½ teaspoon water
Assorted colors of paste food coloring
Small, soft paintbrush

DIRECTIONS

1. In large mixing bowl, beat together butter and shortening. Gradually add sugar, beating until light and fluffy. Add egg mixture.

2. Divide dough into fourths. Shape each fourth into roll, about ½" diameter. Wrap each roll in plastic wrap and refrigerate for 2 to 3 hours.

3. Preheat oven to 375 degrees. Cut dough into ⅛"-thick slices. If dough cracks or crumbles while slicing or shaping, let stand at room temperature for 15 to 30 minutes before using.

4. For each cookie, arrange 15 to 17 slices on an ungreased cookie sheet to resemble rose. Take one slice and roll to make bud; see Diagram A. Attach additional slices to bud by overlapping around and pinching at bottom; see Diagram B. Continue until entire rose is formed; see Diagram C. Pinch excess from bottom if needed.

Diagram A

5. Bake for 7 to 8 minutes. Let cool on wire rack.

6. To prepare Edible Decorator Paint, mix egg yolk with water. Divide mixture into several small cups. Add paste food coloring as desired. If needed, add more water, one drop at time, to make paint consistency of ink. Use thin coats. Allow each color to dry before proceeding with shading color. Find pictures of real roses to refer to when painting cookies.

7. Return cookies to cookie sheet and bake for two minutes to set paint and cook egg yolk. Remove to rack and cool completely. Recipe makes two dozen rose-shaped cookies.

Diagram B

Diagram C

Design A

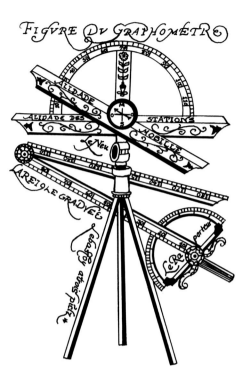

Design B

Design C

FOR THE ADVENTURER

COMPASS BOX

MATERIALS

4¼" x 2¾" wood box with lid
Wood stain
Wood-grain paper
Colored pencils
Tea bag
¼"-thick balsa wood
Hot glue gun and glue sticks
Small compass with 1⅛" dial
Two ½" brass hinges
Brass clasp set
Brass tacks or brads

DIRECTIONS

1. Stain wood box and lid. Let stain dry.

2. Using wood-grain paper, photocopy compass patterns on page 99. Color compass designs with waterproof pencils. Steep tea bag and squeeze moisture out. Rub tea bag lightly over paper to tea-dye compass designs. Let paper dry. When dry, cut each compass design to 4½" x 2½".

3. Cut piece of balsa wood to fit snugly inside lid of box and glue in place. Sand top of balsa wood flush with edges inside lid. Set lid aside.

4. Cut four 1" x ½" balsa wood blocks. Glue each block vertically inside box to right of each corner to form supports; see diagram.

Diagram

5. Cut piece of balsa wood to fit box bottom. Mark center and drill or cut 1" hole. Remove glass cover from compass dial. Insert compass through center hole in balsa wood. Glue compass to balsa wood. Glue balsa wood to box bottom, resting on support blocks.

6. Carefully cut out 1" circle at center of compass Design A to fit exactly over compass dial. (Adjust cutting measurement if compass dial is bigger or smaller than in sample.) Glue Design A over compass dial, making sure all lines inside dial and on outer design are aligned. Replace glass cover.

7. Center and glue compass Design B inside lid. Center and glue compass Design C outside top of lid. Put lid on box.

8. On back of box and lid, space hinges ½" from each side. Attach hinges with tacks. Center brass clasps on front of box and lid. Attach with tacks.

101

FRUIT PINCUSHIONS

MATERIALS (for cushions)

Satin fabric, ⅛ yard each: red,
    peach, yellow, purple;
    matching threads
Scrap of brown fabric;
    matching thread
Ten green silk leaves
10 cups of sawdust
12" length of florist's wire
Tacky glue

DIRECTIONS
All seams are ¼" unless
otherwise indicated.

Apple

1. Make apple wedge and stem
patterns on page 106. From red
satin, cut five wedges. Cut two
stem pieces from brown fabric.

2. Place two apple wedges
together with right sides
facing and raw edges aligned.
Stitch one long edge. Press
seam open. Repeat with three
remaining pieces. To complete
sphere, stitch last seam 1½"
from top and bottom, leaving
center of seam open. Turn.

3. Stuff apple firmly with
sawdust and slipstitch seam
opening closed. Stitch
drawing thread from bottom
of apple to top. Pull top and
bottom toward center; see
Diagram A.

Diagram A

4. Place stem pieces together
with right sides facing and
raw edges aligned. Stitch top,
one side and bottom of stem
using ⅛" seam. Turn. Stuff
stem with sawdust and
slipstitch remaining side
closed.

5. Attach stem to apple and
secure thread. Stitch silk leaf
to top of apple near stem.

Peach

1. Repeat Steps 1–5 of apple,
using peach satin and cutting
five wedges. Do not pull draw
stitch as tightly so shape is
smooth and round. Do not
make stem.

Pear

1. Repeat Steps 1–5 of apple,
using pear pattern and
cutting five wedges from
yellow satin. Stitch drawing
thread from bottom of pear to
each side seam about 1½"
from top; see Diagram B.
Stitch stem to top of pear.

Grapes

1. For grapes, cut twelve 3"
circles and six 1½" circles from
purple satin.

2. Turn raw edges under ¼"
and stitch gathering threads
around outside of each circle.
Stuff and pull thread tightly to
gather circle around stuffing.
Secure threads.

3. Cluster stuffed circles
together and stitch to secure.

4. Cut florist's wire into two 6"
lengths. Wind craft wire
lengths around pencil to make
two vines. Slide wire off
pencil and stretch out slightly.
Glue craft wire and leaves to
grape cluster at top.

Diagram B

FINISHED SIZE

Approximately 2¾" x 7" x 2½".

MATERIALS (for crochet)

Yarn description: Cotton crochet thread (slightly larger than #10), Mauve (A), Pearl Cotton #8, Ecru (B)

Yarn pictured: Rowan Designer Collection, 50-gr., 160 m balls, 3 balls Pale Mauve #311 (A), DMC Pearl Cotton #8, 95 yard ball, 1 ball Ecru.

Tools: Size 7 steel crochet hook; size 18 tapestry needle.

GAUGE

8 sts = 1"
9 rows = 1"

DIRECTIONS

Rnd 1: With A, ch 42, sk 1 ch, sc in next ch, sc in each of next 39 ch, 3 sc in last st, turn, work along other side of ch, sc in each st, 2 sc in same place as beg ch, sl st to beg ch to close.

Rnd 2: Ch 1, 2 sc in next st, sc in each of next 40 sts, 2 sc in next st, sc in next st, 2 sc in next st, sc in each of next 40 sts, 2 sc in next st, sl st to beg ch.

Rnd 3: Ch 1, sc in next st, 2 sc in next st, sc in each of 40 sts, 2 sc in next st, sc in each of next 3 sts, 2 sc in next st, sc in each of next 40 sts, 2 sc in next st, sc in next st, sl st to beg ch.

Rnd 4: Ch 1, sc in each of next 2 sts, 2 sc in next st, sc in each of next 40 sts, 2 sc in next st, sc in each of next 5 sts, 2 sc in next st, sc in each of next 40 sts, 2 sc in next st, sc in each of next 2 sts, sl st to beg ch.

Rnd 5: Ch 1, sc in each of next 3 sts, 2 sc in next st, sc in each of next 40 sts, 2 sc in next st, sc in each of next 7 sts, 2 sc in next st, sc in each of next 40 sts, sc in next 3 sts, sl st to beg ch.

Rnd 6: Cont in this same manner having 2 more sts at each end bet the inc of 2 sc = 9 sts bet inc.

Rnd 7: 11 sts bet inc.

Rnd 8: 13 sts bet inc.

Rnd 9: 15 sts bet inc.

Rnd 10: Cont in this same manner, except work 2 sc in end section, sc in each of next 9 sts, 2 sc in next st, sc in each of next 9 sts, 2 sc in next st = 19 sts in end section, there will be one extra inc.

Rnd 11: Cont as for rnd 6, having 20 sts bet inc.

Rnd 12: 22 sts bet inc = 132 sts around.

Rnd 13: Ch 1, work in back lp only, sc in each st around, sl st to beg ch.

Rnd 14-34: Work in a spiral, mark beg of rnd with a safety pin and move it up a beg of each rnd, sc in each st around, remove safety pin and end last rnd with a sl st in next st. Do not fasten off.

Rim: Rnd 1: Work in front lp only, ch 2, hdc in each st around, sl st to top of beg ch.

Rnds 2-4: Work through both lps, ch 2, hdc in each st around, sl st to top of beg ch. After rnd 4 is complete, fasten off.

Lace Edging:
Rnd 1: Wrong side facing, join B in center st of narrow side of basket rim, * ch 5, sc in next st, (ch 5, sk 1 st, sc in next st) 33 times, rep from * once, end with ch 3, dc in beg ch = 68 lps around.

Rnd 2: Ch 5, sc in same lp, * ch 3, sc in nest lp, 5 sc in next lp, sc in next lp, ch 3, (sc, ch 5, sc) in next lp, rep from * around, ch 3, sl st to beg ch, sl st in next lp.

Rnd 3: * (Ch 3, sc in same lp) 3 times, ch 3, sk next sp and next sc, sc in next 5 sc, ch 3, sk next sc and sp, sc in next lp, rep from * around, omit last sc of last rep, sl st to beg ch, sl st in next ch-3 lp.

Rnd 4: Ch 5, dc in same lp, * ch 2, (dc, ch 2, dc, ch 2, dc) in next lp, ch 2, (dc, ch 2, dc) in next lp, ch 3, sc in center sc of next 5-sc group, ch 3, sk 2 sc and next lp, (dc, ch 2, dc) in next lp, rep from * around, omit last (dc, ch 2, dc) of last rep, sl st to 3rd ch of beg ch. Fasten off.

Handle:
Row 1: With A, ch 51, sk 1 ch, sc in next 50 ch, ch 1, turn.

Rows 2-8: Sc in next 50 sts, ch 1, turn, leave a 36" tail. Fasten off.

Assembly: Whipstitch lengthwise to form a tube. Sew each end of tube handle to center of each long side of basket.

STEM

APPLE/PEACH

PEAR

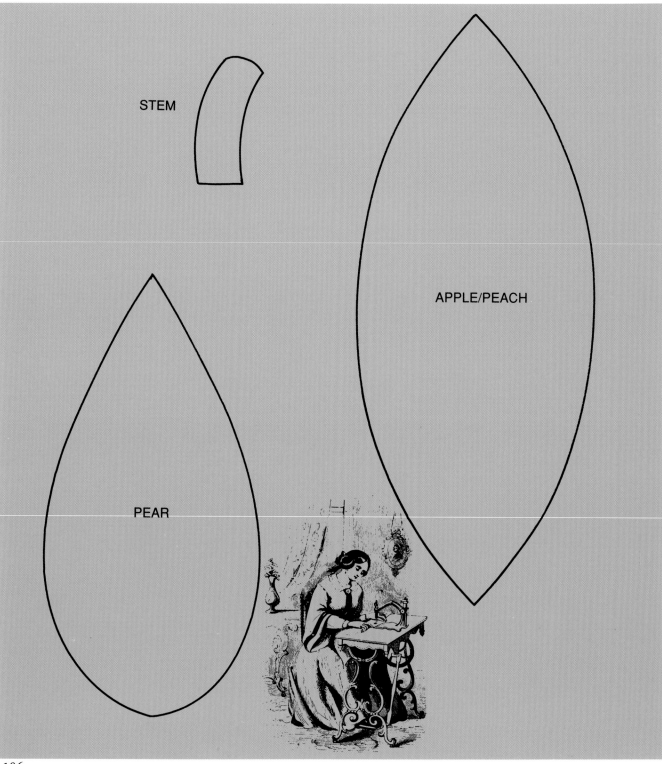

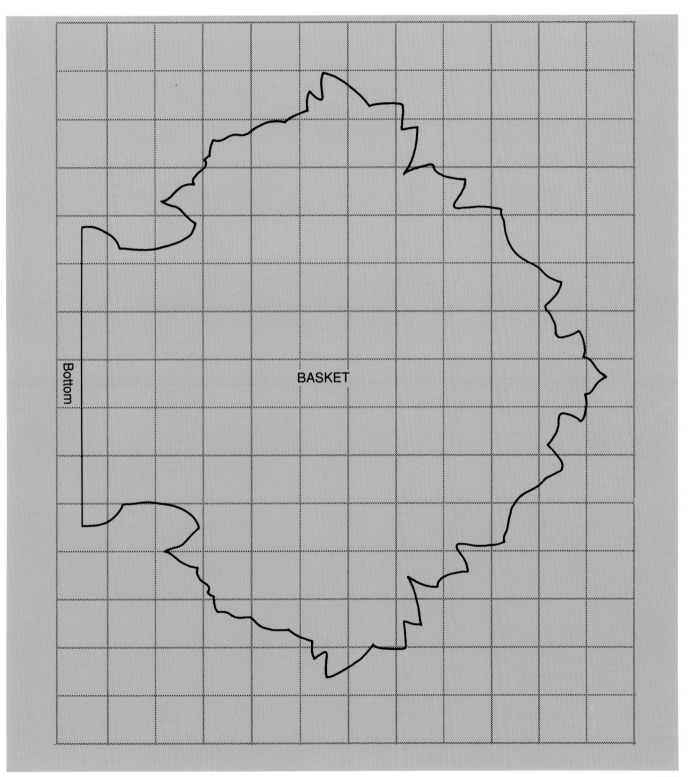

BASKET

Bottom

VICTORIAN BOOKENDS

MATERIALS

Two 15" x 15" x ¾" wood
    pieces
Jigsaw
Fine sandpaper
Ivory acrylic paint
Two L-shaped metal
    bookends
Drill and ¼" metal drill bit
Six flathead screws
2½ yards of ½" pink satin
    ribbon
½" double-sided tape
Victorian catalogs and
    magazines
Decoupage glue
Embossed greeting card
Six dried and pressed pansies
Two cardboard heart-shaped
    gift tags

DIRECTIONS

1. Make flower basket pattern
on page 107 and transfer two
to wood pieces. Cut baskets
with jigsaw. Sand edges.

2. Paint baskets ivory. Let
paint dry.

3. Position bookend against
one side of one wood basket.
Align bottom of bookend with
basket bottom. Mark desired
placement for three screws to
fix bookend to basket. Drill
¾" holes in bookend and
basket at marks. Repeat with
other basket and bookend.

4. Cut ribbon into four 2½"
lengths, four 4" lengths, four
6½" lengths and four 7"
lengths. Attach double-sided
tape to ribbon lengths. Tape
lengths to front bottom of one
basket, making crisscross
pattern; see photograph. Trim
edges. Repeat.

5. Cut pictures and flowers
from catalogs and magazines.
Using decoupage glue, glue
magazine cutouts to top area
of one basket. Cut shapes from
embossed greeting card. Glue
card cutouts, dried pansies
and gift tag to basket. Repeat.

6. Using three screws, attach
bookend to basket. Repeat.

FOR THE DESSERT LOVER

DESSERT COVER

MATERIALS

3½ yards of ⅛" wire
Wire cutters
Soldering iron and solder
6 yards of ½" ivory bias tape
Tacky glue
½ yard of ivory lace with
    4"- square panels
Liquid ravel preventer
Tacky glue
3 yards of ⅛" white rope
Eight ¼" ivory cloth
    pom-poms
Needle and thread
1" ivory cloth flower

DIRECTIONS

1. Cut wire into twenty-four 4" lengths and two 11" lengths.

2. With 11" lengths, make cross, matching centers. Solder at intersection. Solder 4" wire length at one end and, using three additional lengths, make 4" square; see Diagram A.

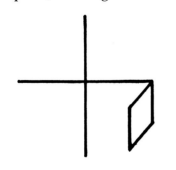

Diagram A

3. Continue soldering remaining 4" wire lengths to make an octagon of squares; see Diagram B.

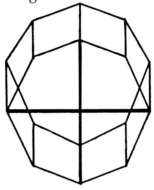

Diagram B

4. Anchor one end of ivory bias tape to one end of top cross wire with glue. Wrap ivory bias tape tightly around all wires, cutting and gluing as needed.

5. Place wire octagon on piece of paper and trace around it with pencil. Pin paper to lace, centering one lace square in middle of pattern. Cut out octagon from lace, applying liquid ravel preventer on raw edges. With tacky glue, attach edges of lace to top of wire octagon.

6. Cut 4" x 32" strip from lace, applying liquid ravel preventer on raw edges. Glue strip around edge of octagon.

7. Cut ivory rope into four 22" lengths. Tie knot in center of one length. With needle and thread, stitch knot to one top corner of octagon. With left end of length and right end of another length, tie bow. Stitch bow to next octagon corner.

8. Tie knot in middle of second length and stitch knot to next corner. Continue tying and stitching bows and knots until rope trims top of octagon.

9. With needle and thread, stitch pom-pom to each tail end of four bows. Stitch cloth flower to top center of lace.

FOR THE TEA PARTY LOVER

FANTASY TEA SET

MATERIALS

Thrift-store cup and saucer
Silk leaves
Newspapers
Green acrylic paint
Paintbrush
Assorted artificial berries
Ten small, silk rosebuds
Twenty-four tiny pinecones
Thrift-store metal teapot
    with lid
Sheet moss
Hot glue gun and glue sticks

DIRECTIONS

1. Place silk leaves on newspaper. Paint green to match moss. Let paint dry.

2. Glue silk leaves on cup, layering leaves to cover entire cup. Fold leaf ends over edge to inside of cup. Decorate cup as desired with berries, rosebuds and pinecones; see photograph.

3. Glue silk leaves on saucer, layering leaves to cover entire saucer. Fold leaf ends underneath saucer.

4. Glue moss over entire teapot and lid. Decorate lid with assorted berries, rosebuds, leaves and pinecones as desired; see photograph.

To: Sara
From: Nate

You've worked to create unique and
cherished gifts. Now, wrap them with flair! Make
tags from ribbons and berries, velvet and glitter,
colored clay or wrapping paper. Use quilted
fabric envelopes to wrap cards glowing with
an abacus tree, brass stars or lavender flowers.
Choose from boxes made of taffeta,
pansies or velvet.

For the Gift-Giver

CHAPTER

6

WRAPPED PRESENT

MATERIALS

Photograph on page 114.

4½" x 3¼" piece of watercolor
  paper
Black or gold fine-tip marker
Small hole punch
½ yard of ⅝" burgundy wired
  ribbon
12" length of 1½" burgundy
  wired ribbon
Silk leaves
Red plastic berries

DIRECTIONS

1. With marker, write names
on watercolor paper. Punch
hole in top left corner.

2. Cut ⅝" ribbon to one 10"
length and one 7" length.
Wrap 10" ribbon length
around tag lengthwise.
Overlap and glue ends on
front of tag about 1" from left
side. Repeat with 7" ribbon
length around width of tag.

3. Glue silk leaves around area
where ribbons cross, covering
ribbon ends. With 1½" ribbon,
tie bow. Glue bow over leaves.
Glue berries around bow and
leaves.

Fabric Envelope

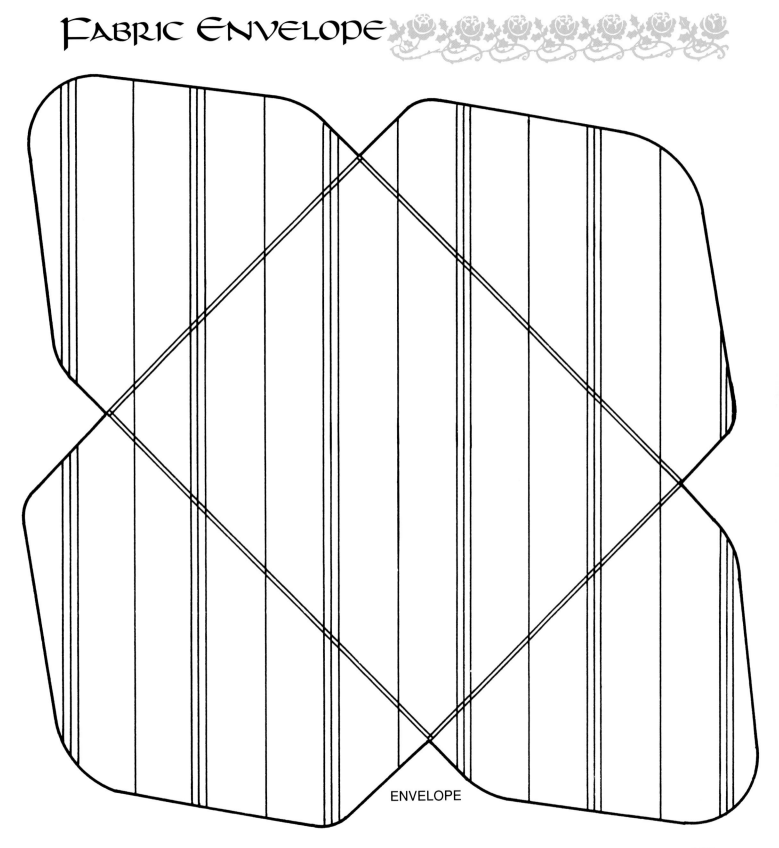

ENVELOPE

FABRIC ENVELOPE

MATERIALS

20" x 24" piece of floral print
  fabric
10" square of contrasting
  fabric; matching thread
Scraps of assorted fabric
Button
Small pearls

DIRECTIONS
All seams are ¼".

*See General Instructions to make
fabric leaves and yo-yos.*

1. Make envelope pattern on
page 117. From floral print
fabric, cut one for lining and
one for front. Also cut 3" x 1"
strip of fabric for button loop.
From contrasting fabric, cut
four 1½" x 8" strips. Cut
twelve 2½" circles from
assorted fabric.

2. With wrong sides facing
and raw edges aligned, stitch
envelope lining and front
along raw edges. To machine
quilt, stitch rows as shown on
pattern. Double-stitch
rectangle in center of fabric;
see pattern.

3. With right sides of bias strip
and envelope front facing,
align raw edges and stitch
around flap to within ½" of
corner. Double-fold bias to
right side of lining. Slipstitch,
tucking raw edges under at
corner. Repeat on remaining
three flaps.

4. Fold side flaps toward
center and tack overlapping
points together. Fold bottom
flap up and slipstitch edges to
side flaps. Center and sew
button 1" from point of
bottom flap.

5. To make loop, fold 3" x 1"
strip of fabric in half
lengthwise. With right sides
facing and raw edges aligned,
stitch long edge. Turn. Insert
one short end inside opposite
short end. Tuck raw edges to
inside and slipstich closed.
Stitch loop to inside point of
top flap.

6. With circles, make eleven
fabric leaves and one yo-yo.

7. On front of top flap attach
fabric leaves and place yo-yo
in center. Stitch pearls around
leaves and one in center of
yo-yo.

VELVET HEARTS

MATERIALS (for one)

10" square of burgundy
    velvet; matching thread
45" of ¼" green silk ribbon
Thirteen porcelain roses
Gold thread
Polyester stuffing
Tacky glue
Fine glitter

DIRECTIONS

All seams are ¼".

1. Make heart pattern. Cut two from velvet.

2. With right sides facing, stitch heart pieces together, leaving an opening. Clip seam allowances at cleavage. Turn. Stuff firmly and slipstitch opening closed.

3. For hanger, thread needle with 10" of gold thread. Run thread through top point of heart. Pull ends to even lengths and tie ends into knot. Trim thread close to knot.

4. Cut green silk ribbon to 1". Roll ends, bring together and glue; see diagram. Repeat to make 45 leaves. Place and glue around heart; see photograph for placement. Glue porcelain hearts on top of leaves.

5. With glue, write receiver's name on heart. Sprinkle fine glitter over top of glue; shake off excess. Let glue dry.

Diagram

HEART

CLAY HEART

MATERIALS

Fimo clay: red, pink, white
Non-waxed dental floss
Card stock paper
Tacky glue
Green acrylic paint
Fine paintbrush
Metallic gold writing pen

DIRECTIONS

1. Knead each color of clay until soft and pliable. Roll red clay into 5"-long, ⅛"-diameter tube. Roll white clay into ¼" x 5" rectangle. Roll white clay around red tube, sealing seam. Roll pink clay into ½" x 5" rectangle. Roll pink clay around red/white tube. Repeat, alternating inside, center and outside colors to make three tubes.

2. Using dental floss, cut clay tubes into ⅛" slices. Bake clay circles according to product instructions.

3. Cut 4½" x 3" card from paper. Position clay circles into heart shape on card. Glue in place. In right bottom corner, position three clay circles and glue.

4. With fine brush, paint leaves close to heart and three corner clay circles; see photograph. Let paint dry.

5. With gold-metallic pen, add accents to clay circles and leaves. Also, write gift information or holiday message.

TREE STAR

MATERIALS

4½" x 3¼" piece of watercolor
  paper
Holiday wrapping paper
Tacky glue
Small hole punch
Textured green paper
12" length of ⅞" gold-trimmed
  wired ribbon
Gold tin star
Gold-metallic pen

DIRECTIONS

*See General Instructions to make
ribbon rosette.*

1. Wrap and glue wrapping
paper to watercolor paper.
Punch hole in top left corner.
Make tree pattern and transfer
to green paper. Cut one tree.
Cut 12" length of gold-
trimmed wired ribbon.

2. With gold-metallic pen,
write names on tree shape.
Glue tree to wrapped tag,
matching bottom straight
edges.

3. With wired ribbon, make
ribbon rosette. Glue rosette to
top of tree. Glue gold star to
center of rosette.

TREE

ABACUS TREE

MATERIALS

7" x 10" piece of green paper
7" x 5" piece of beige paper
1 yard of brass florist's wire
Fifteen green glass seed beads
Seven gold glass bugle beads
Spray adhesive

DIRECTIONS

1. Fold green paper in half, matching short ends. Work with fold at top.

2. Make tree pattern. Center and transfer pattern onto front of card. Cut out tree. Center and transfer pattern onto beige paper. Cut out tree.

3. Using a needle, make holes ¼" apart around tree as shown on pattern.

4. Cut the wire into six 3½" lengths and three 4" lengths. Thread one wire end through one hole. Bend end slightly. Thread beads onto the wire as desired; see photograph. Thread opposite end through opposite hole so that wire is at a diagonal. Repeat with remaining wires and beads. Alternate between leaving wire ends on inside and outside of card. Tape down ends on inside.

5. Spray the inside front of the card with adhesive. Match trees and adhere beige stationery to inside front of card.

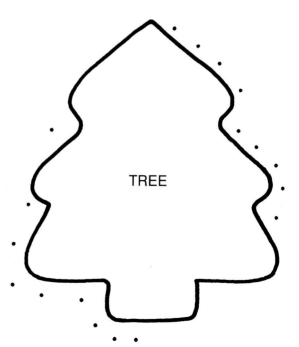

TREE

127

LACY BASKET

MATERIALS

7" x 10" piece of drawing paper
Watercolor paints: blue,
    purple
Paintbrush
12"-square lace-like paper
    napkin
Tacky glue
Tracing paper
Pencil
Carbon paper
Dried small flowers: violet,
    purple
¾ yard of ¾"-wide lavender
    wired ribbon
25 tiny purple/blue glass
    beads

DIRECTIONS

1. Fold drawing paper in half, making short ends meet. Paint front of card blue. Let paint dry.

2. Cut corner of lace paper napkin to make triangle measuring 7" on longest edge. Working with fold at top, glue triangle with point facing down onto front of blue card.

3. Make pattern for basket. Transfer basket design centered on paper napkin triangle. Paint basket on paper napkin purple. Let paint dry.

4. Glue violet and purple flowers to top of painted basket. Tie ribbon into bow. Glue ribbon to card. Glue beads to card. See photograph for placement.

BASKET

BRASS STARS

MATERIALS

7" x 10" piece of corrugated
    paper
7" x 3" piece of green
    handmade paper
7" x 5" piece of beige
    stationery
Red acrylic paint
5" square of brass sheeting
Spray adhesive
Tacky glue
Gold thread
Needle
Ballpoint pen

DIRECTIONS

1. Paint the corrugated paper red on one side. Fold the paper in half, making short ends meet.

2. Tear one long end of green handmade paper to make edge look worn. Using spray adhesive, attach handmade paper strip to top of red card at fold.

3. Cut gold thread into thirty-six 7" lengths. Using twelve gold thread strands, thread through the top left corner of card. Make ¼" stitch and pull the thread through both holes twice. Tie knot in center. Repeat with twelve strands in the center top and twelve in top right corner. See photograph.

4. Trace star pattern. Transfer pattern to brass sheeting using a ballpoint pen. The pen will indent the pattern. Cut out three stars with scissors. With tacky glue, attach stars to card front as desired.

5. Spray adhesive on inside back of card. Adhere stationery piece.

STAR

TAFFETA BOXES

MATERIALS

2 yards of iridescent taffeta
1 yard of fleece
Gold-metallic thread
Thin gold-metallic cording
1 yard of 1" gold ribbon

DIRECTIONS (for one)

All seams are ¼" and visible.

This easy project goes especially fast using an overlock machine. Otherwise, finish all edges with a zigzag or satin stitch.

1. From taffeta, cut 12 squares, each measuring 6" x 6". From fleece, cut six 5½" x 5½" squares. Cut cording into eight 18" lengths. Cut ribbon into two 18" lengths and cut small Vs at ends.

2. To make box sides, sandwich and center fleece piece between wrong sides of six pairs of taffeta squares. Stack two squares together. With raw edges aligned, zigzag or satin stitch one edge of two squares. Open out. Repeat with two more squares, making strip of four squares with seams showing on outside; see Diagram A. Stitch last square to first, completing box with open top; see Diagram B. Finish three top edges of three side pieces of box.

3. For crisp corners, attach bottom square to box by stitching one edge of square, stopping at corners, then stitching opposite edge. Stitch remaining two opposite edges.

4. For lid, finish three edges of top square. Stitch remaining edge to top unfinished edge of box. Thread two pieces of 18" cording through one unattached corner of lid. Secure cording to lid with half knot in center of cording. Knot ends of cording. Repeat on opposite corner of lid and front corners of box. On two corners of lid, tie cording around center of 18" ribbon lengths. To secure lid, tie cording and ribbon lengths into bows at corners.

Diagram B

Diagram A

PANSY BOX

MATERIALS

6"-square cardboard box
    with lid
Acrylic paints: rust, dark
    brown
Small sponges
Floral greeting cards
Thick, high-gloss lacquer
Small bowl to hold lacquer
Tacky glue

DIRECTIONS

1. Using sponge, paint box
and lid dark brown. Let paint
dry. Sponge-paint box and lid
lightly with rust, using paint
sparingly to create an
antiqued look.

2. Cut flowers desired from
old greeting cards.

3. Pour small amount of
lacquer in bowl. Dip flowers
in lacquer and let dry for 10 to
15 minutes. Dip second time.
Let dry for 24 hours.

4. Glue coated flowers to box
lid. Drip some lacquer around
edges of flowers to give them
an embossed look. Let lacquer
dry.

VELVET BAGS

MATERIALS (for two bags)

⅜ yard of green and purple
    velvet; matching thread
    for both
1½ yards of ⅛" metallic gold
    cording
Miniature wooden holly
    leaves and stars
Steam iron

DIRECTIONS
All seams are ½".

1. Cut one 12" x 15" piece each of green and purple velvet. To imprint holly leaves on green piece, group wooden leaves as desired on ironing board. Place velvet, right side down, over leaves; steam iron. To avoid displacing leaves, do not move iron rapidly. Allow fabric to cool. Repeat for purple velvet, using wooden stars.

2. To make green velvet bag, fold right side of top 12" edge of green velvet piece over ½"; zigzag stitch. Fold velvet in half with side 15" edges aligned, and right sides facing. Stitch; press seam open. With seam centered, stitch remaining bottom 12" raw edge. Pinch corners 1" from bottom seam; see diagram. Stitch corners. Turn. Repeat, to make purple bag.

3. Stuff bags as desired. Cut metallic gold cording in half; knot ends. Wrap one cording length around each bag; tie ends in bow to secure.

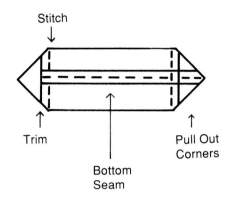

Diagram

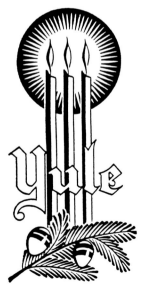

General Instructions

Bullion Leaf/Petal Stitch

1. Using one strand of embroidery floss, bring needle up at 1, down at 2, with loose stitch. Bring needle tip out again at 1; do not pull needle completely through fabric; see Diagram A.

2. Wrap loose-stitched floss around needle tip about thirteen times. Holding finger over coiled floss, pull needle through wrapped floss; see Diagram B. Insert needle again at 2, pulling to fabric back. If desired, pull floss slightly to curve bullion petal; see Diagram C.

3. To form rose, stitch petals in close groups.

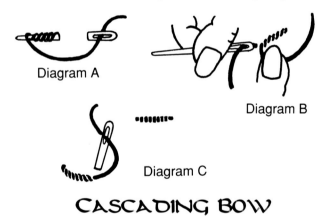

Diagram A

Diagram B

Diagram C

Cascading Bow

With ribbon length, tie small bow. Thread needle with tails. Stitch ribbon length to fabric very loosely, twisting ribbon between each stitch; see diagram. Place stitches as desired.

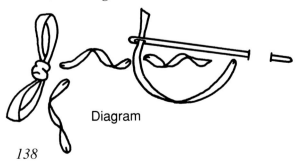

Diagram

Crochet Tips

ABBREVIATIONS:

beg	begin(ning)
bet	between
ch	chain
ch-	chain previously made
cont	continue(d) (ing)
dc	double crochet
dec	decrease(s) (d) (ing)
dtr	double triple crochet
ea	each
est	establish(ed)
hdc	half double crochet
inc	increase(s) (d) (ing)
lp(s)	loop(s)
prev	previous
rem	remain(s) (ing)
rep	repeat
rnd(s)	round(s)
sc	single crochet
sk	skip
sl st	slipstitch
sp(s)	space(s)
st(s)	stitch(es)
tog	together
tr cr	triple crochet
yo	yarn over

GAUGE: Before beginning project, work 4"-square-gauge swatch using recommended-size hook. Measure 1" or 2" (as given in the gauge note); count and compare number of stitches in swatch with designer's gauge. If there are fewer stitches in gauge swatch, try smaller hook; if there are more stitches, try larger hook.

HOLDING HOOK: Hold hook like a pencil or piece of chalk. If hook has finger rest, position thumb and opposing finger there for extra control. Weave yarn through fingers of left hand to control amount of yarn fed into work and provide tension. Once work has begun, thumb and middle finger of left hand come into play, pressing together to hold stitches just made.

CROSS-STITCH TIPS

CROSS-STITCH: Make one cross-stitch for each symbol on chart. Bring needle up at A, down at B, up at C, down at D; see diagram. For rows, stitch across fabric from left to right to make half-crosses and then back to complete stitches.

FABRICS: Designs in this book are worked on even-weave fabrics made especially for cross-stitch, which can be found in most needlework shops. Fabrics used for models are identified in sample information by color, name and thread count per inch.

PREPARING FABRIC: Cut fabric at least 3" larger on all sides than finished design size or cut as indicated in sample information to ensure enough space for project assembly. To keep fabric from fraying, whipstitch or machine zigzag along raw edges or apply liquid ravel preventer.

NEEDLES: Choose needle that will slip easily through fabric holes without piercing fabric threads. For fabric with 11 or fewer threads per inch, use needle size 24; for 14 threads per inch, use needle size 24 or 26; for 18 or more threads per inch, use needle size 26. Never leave needle in design area of fabric. It may leave rust or permanent impression on fabric.

FINISHED DESIGN SIZE: To determine size of finished design, divide stitch count by number of threads per inch of fabric. When design is stitched over two threads, divide stitch count by half the threads per inch.

FLOSS: Use 18" lengths of floss. For best coverage, separate strands. Dampen with wet sponge. Then put back together number of strands called for in color code.

STITCHING METHOD: For smooth stitches, use push-and-pull method. Starting on wrong side of fabric, bring needle straight up, pulling floss completely through to right side. Re-insert needle and bring it back straight down, pulling needle and floss completely through to back of fabric. Keep floss flat but do not pull thread tight. For even stitches, tension should be consistent throughout.

FABRIC BOW

This bow can be made from ribbon, eliminating Step 2.

1. Cut fabric 1½" x 6". Press long edges, top and bottom, ¼" to wrong side.

2. Fold fabric in half, short edges aligned; mark center. Press. Fold short raw edges into center, end over end, overlapping ¼".

3. Stitch gathering thread at center mark. Pull thread tightly to gather. Wrap thread around stitches to secure. Cover stitching with small fabric or ribbon square.

FABRIC LEAF/FLOWER PETAL

Press 2" fabric circle in half with raw edges aligned. With folded edge up, fold into thirds, overlapping sides. Stitch gathering thread on raw edge; see diagram. Gather tightly. Wrap and tie thread around stitches to secure.

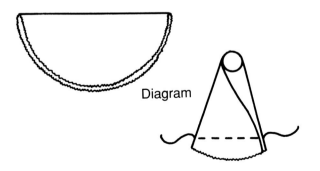

Diagram

FRENCH KNOT

Using one strand of embroidery floss or ribbon length, bring needle up at 1. Wrap floss/ribbon around needle two times. Insert needle short distance from 1, pulling floss/ribbon until it fits snugly around needle; see diagram. Pull needle through to back, leaving knot.

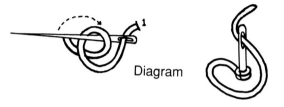

Diagram

FABRIC ROSE

1. Fold fabric strip in half lengthwise with long, raw edges aligned. For crisper rose, press fabric.

2. Fold fabric ends at right angles. Stitch gathering thread on long raw edge, leaving needle and thread attached; see Diagram A.

3. Slightly gather fabric, simultaneously wrapping to make flower. Force needle through lower fabric edge; see Diagram B. Secure thread and trim excess. Fluff.

Diagram A

Diagram B

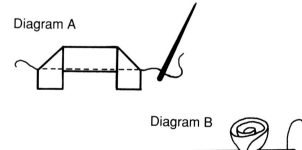

FERN STITCH

Using ribbon length or embroidery floss, work from top to bottom of frond, bringing needle up at 1, down at 2; see diagram. Bring needle up at 3, down at 1. Bring needle up at 4, down again at 1. Then, bring needle up at 5, down at 1. Bring needle up at 6, down at 5. Repeat, until desired length is stitched.

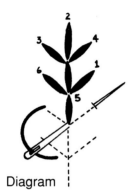

Diagram

LAZY-DAISY LEAF/BUD STITCH

Using one strand of embroidery floss for leaf and one ribbon length for bud, bring needle up at 1, down at 2, with loose stitch; see diagram. Bring needle up on one side of floss / ribbon at 3, then back through fabric on opposite side at 4. A bud is often finished at 1 and 2 by making French knot.

Diagram

RIBBON LEAF

1. Fold ribbon length in half lengthwise, with wired edges aligned. Turn folded ribbon corners up to within ⅛" from wired edge.

2. Stitch gathering thread along bottom edges; see Diagram A. Gather; secure ends. Open and shape leaf by pulling back short ends until they meet; see Diagram B. Secure.

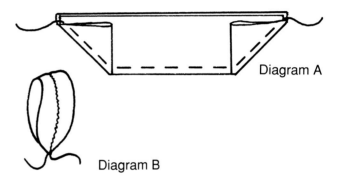

Diagram A

Diagram B

RIBBON PENCIL DAISY

1. Holding two pencils 1" apart, loop ribbon length back-and-forth, over-and-under, alternating pencils. Loosely stitch gathering thread between pencils. Gather tightly. Wrap thread around stitches to secure; see diagram.

2. Remove pencils, fluff and separate petal loops.

Diagram

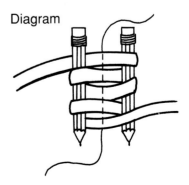

RIBBON ROSETTES

1. For ¼" rosette, cut 5" ribbon length. For ½" rosette, cut 9" length. Mark center of ribbon length. Beginning at one end, fold one end forward at right angle. Holding vertical length, begin rolling ribbon at fold horizontally to form bud; see Diagram A.

2. Then, fold horizontal ribbon backward at right angle and continue rolling bud, aligning top edges of bud to second fold and rounding corner; see Diagram B.

3. Continue folding ribbon backward at right angles and rolling bud to center mark. Secure, leaving needle and thread attached.

4. Stitch gathering thread on bottom edge of remaining ribbon half. Gather tightly. Wrap gathered ribbon around bud. Secure and fluff flower.

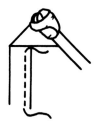

Diagram A   Diagram B

YO-YOS

Fold raw edges of 2½" fabric circle under ¼", stitching gathering thread on outer edge. Gather tightly. Knot ends to secure. Slightly flatten puckered circle, pressing tightened gather inward. Smooth side is bottom and gathered side top; see diagram.

Diagram

METRIC EQUIVALENCY CHART

MM-Millimetres   CM-Centimetres

INCHES TO MILLIMETRES AND CENTIMETRES

INCHES	MM	CM	INCHES	CM	INCHES	CM
⅛	3	0.3	9	22.9	30	76.2
¼	6	0.6	10	25.4	31	78.7
⅜	10	1.0	11	27.9	32	81.3
½	13	1.3	12	30.5	33	83.8
⅝	16	1.6	13	33.0	34	86.4
¾	19	1.9	14	35.6	35	88.9
⅞	22	2.2	15	38.1	36	91.4
1	25	2.5	16	40.6	37	94.0
1¼	32	3.2	17	43.2	38	96.5
1½	38	3.8	18	45.7	39	99.1
1¾	44	4.4	19	48.3	40	101.6
2	51	5.1	20	50.8	41	104.1
2½	64	6.4	21	53.3	42	106.7
3	76	7.6	22	55.9	43	109.2
3½	89	8.9	23	58.4	44	111.8
4	102	10.2	24	61.0	45	114.3
4½	114	11.4	25	63.5	46	116.8
5	127	12.7	26	66.0	47	119.4
6	152	15.2	27	68.6	48	121.9
7	178	17.8	28	71.1	49	124.5
8	203	20.3	29	73.7	50	127.0

YARDS TO METRES

YARDS	METRES	YARDS	METRES	YARDS	METRES	YARDS	METRES	YARDS	METRES
⅛	0.11	2⅛	1.94	4⅛	3.77	6⅛	5.60	8⅛	7.43
¼	0.23	2¼	2.06	4¼	3.89	6¼	5.72	8¼	7.54
⅜	0.34	2⅜	2.17	4⅜	4.00	6⅜	5.83	8⅜	7.66
½	0.46	2½	2.29	4½	4.11	6½	5.94	8½	7.77
⅝	0.57	2⅝	2.40	4⅝	4.23	6⅝	6.06	8⅝	7.89
¾	0.69	2¾	2.51	4¾	4.34	6¾	6.17	8¾	8.00
⅞	0.80	2⅞	2.63	4⅞	4.46	6⅞	6.29	8⅞	8.12
1	0.91	3	2.74	5	4.57	7	6.40	9	8.23
1⅛	1.03	3⅛	2.86	5⅛	4.69	7⅛	6.52	9⅛	8.34
1¼	1.14	3¼	2.97	5¼	4.80	7¼	6.63	9¼	8.46
1⅜	1.26	3⅜	3.09	5⅜	4.91	7⅜	6.74	9⅜	8.57
1½	1.37	3½	3.20	5½	5.03	7½	6.86	9½	8.69
1⅝	1.49	3⅝	3.31	5⅝	5.14	7⅝	6.97	9⅝	8.80
1¾	1.60	3¾	3.43	5¾	5.26	7¾	7.09	9¾	8.92
1⅞	1.71	3⅞	3.54	5⅞	5.37	7⅞	7.20	9⅞	9.03
2	1.83	4	3.66	6	5.49	8	7.32	10	9.14

143

INDEX

Abacus tree 127
Adventurer, For the 101
Afghan, cross-stitch 35
Antique oval fan 23
Apple, ribbon 50
Apron 15
Art Connoisseur, For the 9
Aunt, For Our Egg-centric 89
Baskets 41, 61
Bookends 109
Books, For the Lover of 109
Bottle labels 41
Box, compass 101
Box, supply 32
Box, trinket 21
Boxes 21, 32, 64, 101, 133, 135, 137
Brass stars 131
Caddy 15
Cards 127, 129, 131
Chair, quilted 17
Clay heart 123
Coasters, Needlepoint 81
Collector, For the 51
Compass box 101
Cookies 98
Cooking basket 61
Couturiere, For the 103
Crochet 35, 85, 103
Cross-stitch 35, 64, 81
Cross-stitch afghan 35
Daughter, For Our 73
Dear Friend, For Our 70
Decorated journal 11
Desk set 59
Dessert cover 111
Dessert Lover, For the 111
Dolls 73, 91

Egg, ribbon 89
Fabric envelope 119
Family and Friends, For Our 69
Fans 23, 26, 28
Fantasy tea set 113
Father, For Our 79
Firestarters, pinecone 34
Fisherman, For the 32
Friend, For Our Dear 70
Fruit pincushions 103
Garden Party Lover, For the 41
Gardener, For the 47
General Instructions 138
Gift-Giver, For the 115
Goblets, painted 79
Gourmet Cook, For the 61
Granddaughter, For Our 91
Handkerchief doll 91
Hat box 85
Hunter, For the 35
Journal, decorated 11
Lacy basket 129
Lady, For the Victorian 23
Lawyer, For the 59
Learned, For the 49
Metric Chart 143
Mirror 85
Mother, For Our 85
Musician, For the 21
Needlework, For the Lover of 64
Outdoors Enthusiast, For the 31
Paintbrushes 15
Painter, For the 15
Pansy box 135
Pastry Pundit, For the 98
Photo frame 70
Picnic basket 41

Pincushions, fruit 103
Pinecone firestarters 34
Poet, For the 17
Porcelain doll 73
Purple button fan 28
Quilted stockings 77
Quilted chair 17
Ribbon apple 50
Ribbon egg 89
Ribbon stocking 95
Ribbonwork 23, 26, 28, 50, 70, 89, 95
Romantic, For the 97
Rose cookies 98
Santa stocking 51
Sewing box 64
Son, For Our 77
Stenciled throw 10
Stockings 51, 77, 95
Supply box 32
Taffeta boxes 133
Tags 116, 121, 123, 125
Tea Party Lover, For the 113
Tea set, fantasy 113
Teacher, For the 50
Throw, stenciled 10
Tree star 125
Trinket box 21
Velvet bags 137
Velvet hearts 121
Victorian bookends 109
Victorian Lady, For the 23
Watering cans 47
Wax seals 62
Wrapped present 116
Writer, For the 10

Merry Christmas to all and to all a good night!